Ruth Vaughn

RUTH VAUGHN
and ANITA HIGMAN

Who Will I Be FOR THE Rest OF My Life

w/ Love
to Women
I love

BETHANY HOUSE PUBLISHERS
MINNEAPOLIS, MINNESOTA 55438

Who Will I Be for the Rest of My Life?
Copyright © 1998
Ruth Vaughn and Anita Higman

Cover design by the Lookout Design Group

Scripture quotations identified KJV are from the King James Version
of the Bible.

Scripture quotations identified NKJV are from the New King James
Version of the Bible. Copyright © 1979, 1980, 1982, by Thomas
Nelson, Inc., Publishers. Used by permission. All rights reserved.

Scripture quotations identified TLB are from the Living Bible © 1971
owned by assignment by Illinois Regional Bank N.A. (as trustee). Used
by permission of Tyndale House Publishers, Inc. Wheaton, IL 60189.
All rights reserved.

Published by Bethany House Publishers
A Ministry of Bethany Fellowship International
11400 Hampshire Avenue South
Minneapolis, Minnesota 55438
www.bethanyhouse.com

Printed in the United States of America by
Bethany Press International, Minneapolis, Minnesota 55438

Library of Congress Cataloging-in-Publication Data

CIP data applied for

ISBN 0-7642-2144-2   CIP

For
Bob and Peter,
lovingly using Robert Browning's words:

Grow old with me.
The best is yet to be,
the last of life,
for which the first was made.

RUTH VAUGHN has thirty-nine books to her credit and is still writing. She has also been a playwright and professor of creative writing and drama. Vaughn has an M.A. from the University of Kansas and a Ph.D. from American University. She has two grown sons, and she and her husband, Bob, make their home in Oklahoma City.

ANITA HIGMAN is an avid writer—the author of six books, with four more in the works. She has a B.A. in speech communication and psychology from Southern Nazarene University in Oklahoma. She makes her home in Houston, Texas, with her husband, Peter, and two children.

CONTENTS

Introduction

RUTH VAUGHN

Twenty years ago, I wrote,

Forty candles? Me?
Can't be!
And yet . . .
In forty years,
I have knowledge of success
and
of defeat.
Life is more arduous
Than I had dreamed.

In many ways I have the gold cup,
the top rung of the ladder . . .
a magical, musical carousel
of fulfilling life . . .
yet
in many ways I know
there has to be *more!*
There will be
other cups . . .

other ladders . . .
other carousels . . .

What will the future bring?

I'm frightened.
I'm bewildered.
I'm confused.
I didn't intend to have
forty birthday candles on my cake
NOW!
So soon!

Forty!
I thought Forty was final fulfillment!

I discover
I am only the rough draft
of what I mean to become. . . .

They tell me I'm "over-the-hill."
They tell me I'm becoming obsolete.
They tell me this is the Best Draft
of what I can become. . . .

They tell me . . .
and
they sing sympathy songs,
they laugh that *I am growing old*!

I don't understand this silliness.

I'm in my prime.
Don't they know that
I shall be forever young?!
I shall be forever-forty!
Won't I?

The answer, of course, was NO! To my astonishment . . . I grew from forty to fifty to sixty . . . yes!!! In August my birthday cake had *sixty candles!*

My intuition of *Change* was valid on my fortieth birthday twenty years ago.

There have been new cups, including the chalice of *sorrow.*

There have been new ladders, including those going *down.*

There have been new carousels, including those that burned before my anguished eyes. . . .

My whirling carousel at age forty included marriage, two sons, many publishing feats, a position as professor of creative writing and drama at Southern Nazarene University, occasional stints of flying through the nation for public speaking or drama performances. The music rushed through my life like a flitting, flirting breeze, and I would jump on the whirling horses of achievement, dashing from one to another, landing on my toes to dance . . . dance in the whooshing excitement of being alive, feeling immortal, certain that summer would last forever!

When I was thirty-eight, an eighteen-year-old girl jumped onto my magical carousel. Her name was Anita Breitling. I loved her instantly. I rejoiced in her, often spellbound by her dark-eyed dynamism, her beautiful, expressive face, her sparkling wit, her singing laughter, her dramatic flair with words. She *joyed* my life.

On campus, where she often starred center stage, and in my home, where she often relaxed and played chess with my youngest son, I loved her with a wistful heart. . . . I dreamed her dreams . . . I prayed her prayers. Anita, at eighteen, was hybrid . . . half woman, half child . . . and sometimes neither; only a yearning soul held in the plodding present, reaching for stars, aching for fulfillment, dreaming of creating her own magical carousel.

Now that dream has come true.

At age forty, she is wife to the wonderful Peter Higman, mother to adorable Scott and Hillary, professional author of dramas, news-paper columns, television scripts, and six books.

Anita Breitling Higman has arrived!

People looking on applaud her gold cup . . . her top rung on the ladder . . . her multicolored singing carousel . . . and they celebrate, shouting, "At age forty, she has it all!"

And yet, as I did long ago, Anita knows better. She wrote to me,

· · · · · ·

MODDY,

As you know . . . I'm preparing to blast into age forty in a couple of weeks. What is this raw fear? Or maybe it's an emotional mixed bag of numbness and intense introspection. I am supposed to have "arrived" now in so many ways, but I still feel like a little kid fumbling with marbles on the playground. I don't have the solid confidence I'm told comes with this age.

Oh, I act the part expected of me! My hair, dress, makeup, carriage, spell success. I say the words I know people want to hear. I feel like an actor playing a role.

I'm tired of the show, Moddy. Do other women feel this way sometimes . . . or am I alone . . . *feeling fear of forty*?!

It seems instead of growing up, I've grown older, feeling more ignorant of life than when I was fourteen . . . more fearful of the future! I look in the mirror and I see my own face betraying me with a sadness, a tiredness I can't seem to cover with eyeglasses or makeup. I walk in the peopled world with a bright smile, Moddy, but the second they're past me and I'm alone, my face droops down again, like the image I see in the mirror. I don't know if I'm worn out because I'm getting older . . . or . . . just tired of pretending to have the emotional and spiritual maturity that is reputed to be *REAL* upon reaching the Big 4–0.

Won't you help me?
I feel so alone . . . and so afraid. . . .

• • • • • •

Now approaching the night of forty blazing candles on her February birthday cake, Anita Higman has reached to me for help. The reason for these letters cumulating into stacks is the intimate relationship we have established between us.

Transcending academics, we learned to love so deeply, we "adopted" each other. I do not replace her mother; she is not my birth child. Yet we are *more than friends.* I call her "daughter," and she uses the special love-name my sons gave me when they were children, "Moddy." She lives in Houston, Texas; I live in Oklahoma City, yet our hearts are bonded in family love.

Anita is astonished she is *forty*!

I am astonished I am *sixty*! I never intended to be! Only my parents and elderly people could be sixty—or so I thought—until they placed sixty candles on my birthday cake!

I look at Anita's scribbled letter and move into time warp, back to when my birthday candles glowed forty. I assumed I was the only one frightened of forty. I whispered occasional bits to God, but never once did I tell a single syllable of my stomach-churning concerns to another person. Never once.

I had no one to share my feelings, my frustrations, my fears, stimulated by forty birthday candles on a cake. I handled them alone.

Anita need not face her Forty-Fears alone.
At age sixty, I am here for her.

• • • • • •

In writing these letters it occurred to us that you might like to share our correspondence as you, too, begin to consider . . . or remember . . . forty candles ablaze on your birthday cake . . . and wish

you could articulate the Forty-Feelings,
the Forty-Frustrations,
the Forty-Fears
to a woman "who has been there" and survived
two decades beyond . . .
to a woman who would hold your hand in understanding . . .
to a woman who would share, understand
your failures as well as your successes,
your weaknesses as well as your strengths,
your ignorance as well as your wisdom.

Anita and I invite you to read our mail in this significant season of life.

You are most welcome!

Facing Forty

ANITA HIGMAN

I looked in the mirror today.

I didn't just glance to fluff my hair. I gave myself a good, long look. First, I cocked my head for a general assessment. Then I leaned in for the scarier, unforgiving version of my own reflection.

For the first time, it was a forty-year-old face staring back at me. A smidgen of cheek sag . . . a bit of something turkeylike beginning on my neck . . . and some forehead frown lines all staking their claim on this once-unmarred facial frontier.

Not only was I wondering what was happening to this face, I wondered who was behind those tired eyes. Was I growing up and old at the same time? I didn't see enough answers in the questioning eyes staring back at me.

I guess it was a moment many women experience at this cross-roads of life . . . *a moment of quiet screams.*

• • • • • •

DEAREST MODDY,

Today happened. My fortieth birthday! I am forty years OLD!

For years I've watched middle age circle above me like a vulture, ready to nip at me to see if I'm half dead yet. I've been ready for a Birthday Panic. I knew I was supposed to have a crisis point, so I figured I'd just go ahead and schedule one in.

Then God played a delightful trick on me. I had to postpone my crisis because He plopped a dream-come-true down on my birthday. I wrote and produced my first children's television show and the taping of the program happened TODAY! I whirled around with excitement and had no time whatsoever to be depressed. Then as that wonderment was closing down, my dear husband swept me off to the most romantic restaurant in Houston. It has been a beautiful day in so many ways. One that I shall never forget.

BUT . . .

Now the day is nearly over. My kids and my husband are asleep. I came downstairs to the kitchen to have a cup of Earl Grey tea and a quiet little writing chat with you.

Realistically, Moddy, I know that many of my days will not be as glorious as today. In a few minutes when the clock strikes midnight, the party-pretty day will be over. The dainty petit-four cakes are all eaten, and the balloons are already sagging. I am now truly, in a more profound sense, *facing forty*. Or should I say, *it* is facing me like a well-aimed shotgun on a helpless quail. And I am that helpless quail!

Funny how you can have a splendid, sunshiny day, and then when the house is silent, the dark of night comes to play cruel mind games on a person . . . like me! The house threatens to smother me in its tomblike quietness while I painstakingly conjure up every morbid thought possible. Would you like to hear a few?

Yes, at forty, I am faced with the Big Stuff. When you're thirty, you get perhaps a sensory twinge of what's coming down the aging pike, but you sure can smell it coming at forty! I can sense illness, wrinkles, death of older relatives, friends, and the biggest one . . . *The Unknown*. Oh, I hate that one the most! It means there are no guarantees that I will continue to live a fairy tale. It means I will most likely never write a play that will merit a production on Broadway.

I may not learn to juggle or play the piano very well, and there's a good chance I won't ever get over my food allergies so that I can eat whatever I want and not worry about bloated glands.

I am overwhelmed with new things to face.

Forty! It's an age I don't like at all! I am fighting it! I am not proud of that fact, but I am most certainly not leaning into its possible realities. I do not like the clearer picture of what could loom in the future. I know a lot of people say, "Just enjoy it! As long as you have your health!"

That is a goofy thing to say, really, because a lot of middle-aged people don't have their health. Many of them are on the verge of losing it. They are lining the doctors' offices with every painful ailment known to man.

Moddy, you know I am a big cackling chicken. I just have never been too big on pain. I try at all costs to avoid it. But then, who isn't really somewhat of a coward? I mean, who would rush up to a carnival booth to have their big toe walloped with a sledgehammer? I would personally be concerned about their mental well-being if they decided it might be an interesting idea.

But that is what is expected of all of us, isn't it, Moddy? We are all seemingly forced into this Russian roulette of physical maladies. The older we get, the fewer clicks we have left on the trigger. And our chances for wellness become simply less likely. Until one day . . . *Bang!* The gun goes off! And disease is not shooting blanks. It is a brutal fact of our fallen nature.

Enough about body-pain worries. I haven't even fully figured out who I am yet. So this is sort of a nonperson going around worrying about body pain!

Fortunately, I do know the basics. I know my name, the facts about my life, what I like and don't like. I know that I am a mom and a wife, a Christian, a friend, a writer, and a citizen.

After forty years, I definitely know enough about me to know what I like.

One of the things I love to do most in this world is to hold my children in our rocking chair and just enjoy being close to them. Even though *being with my family* squeals at the top of my giddy list, I also relish trips to my hairdresser, as well as consuming anything and everything made of chocolate. I adore fishing and lilacs and a good romantic movie. But, once again, all of this is more what I like, not *who I am*.

I am a writer, but what if the writer in me never publishes again? Then who am I? I am no longer Anita, the writer. What if my friends abandon me? I am no longer Anita, the woman who has loving friends. Who am I then, really?

I am facing forty with a lot more questions than answers!

Oh, Moddy, I sit in the middle of this dimly lit kitchen seeing only spooky shadows. Just like when I was a kid in my bed at night. Only then I could simply turn on the light. All was well. No hideous monsters. Now when I turn on the kitchen light, the dark glimmers of *The Unknown* remain. Perhaps someday I will be the scary monster with a ragged face and a bitter tongue to match! And maybe I still won't know who I am, except for this hideous description of myself.

In my youth, time was the cute tick-ticking of a cartoon watch. Now time is like Big Ben gonging IN MY FACE. I really don't want to accept the second half of life in resignation to what aging defines. Part of me feels like giving up already, and the other half feels fighting mad. But I would only be fighting Providence, and we both know how futile that is.

Please forgive me for blasting you on this strange, bittersweet night. And thank you for letting me say whatever comes across my brain. That means so much to me. To be able to explode, and to know you are there in loving attendance, picking up the pieces, helping me put myself back together, is part of what makes this life not so difficult. Thank you for loving me unconditionally.

But I'm scared tonight, Moddy, frightened to death of The Unknown four decades ahead of me. These first four have been the adventure of climbing My Mountain, but will the next four hurl me into cruel chasms below?

I know I'm silly, in a way, because I observe people aged eighty climbing higher mountains with vigor, happiness, and greater and greater triumphs. But I'm silly only *in a way*, because I also know people aged eighty drooling in their wheelchairs, helpless to care for their most basic needs.

I've just put my head on the table and wept my painful terrors on my fortieth birthday, where the shotgun of The Unknown forty years ahead of me is well aimed, in its place, ready for its explosion. Where, how, when will be the blast? . . . Will the horror of night become the reality of day? If so, then what is left? Who is left? Or is there the slightest chance my happy life will simply continue on to greater joys, relatively free of pain?

Oh, Moddy, please sit in the ashes with me and let me hold your small but strong hand. And please offer me some advice to decode this scrambled mess of fevered fears.

Did you ever experience this night-terror when you turned forty . . . or maybe at fifty . . . or sixty? As a teenager, my memories of you on a university campus, and my observation of you in the years I grew to be forty, give only a collage of you rushing about confident, achieving, with that everlasting smile and lilting laughter. Even though I knew there were bad times, everyone said you seemed the same. Were you always strong? Did you always smile? Did you ever experience fright in the night . . . or am I the only one . . . *in history*?

Moddy, you loved me when I was your silly teenager. . . . Will you love me tonight when I am your helpless quail?

—Anita

I'm Here for You

RUTH VAUGHN

My house had been filled with laughing teens. As the last car drove away with the shouting, silly good-byes, I thanked God for His goodness in allowing these beloved youth to sparkle my house with their confetti of high-school jokes and their most recent adventures—dramatically presented with Antwon's inimitable comedic skills. *He might replace Jay Leno one day*, I pondered as I went to the mailbox.

At the bottom of the stack of letters was the familiar rainbow envelope arriving from my amazing Anita! I ripped it open. Having just come from the giggling, clowning hours with my young friends, my eyes were prepared to speed-read through Anita's joys, but quickly my eyes halted. *I went back to the beginning.* I stood in the middle of the circular drive reading slowly, because her words agitated emotions into a thundering spin-cycle coming unexpectedly from the secret caverns of my heart.

There was so much I needed to write to this dark-eyed child.

• • • • • •

MY DEAREST "HELPLESS QUAIL" . . .

I have just finished reading your letter and have taken it with me to the computer. I am laughing through my tears. My dear, dramatic Anita, I will "sit in the ashes with you, hold your hand, and do my best to give you words" that might help "decode the scrambled mess of fevered fears." I can only try.

I laugh through tears in the wonder of understanding every syllable of your letter that could have been written by my dramatic hand—not only at age forty, fifty, or sixty, but dozens of nights in between.

I laugh through tears in the joy of your memory-collage filled with mental snapshots of my "rushing about confident, achieving, with that everlasting smile and lilting laughter." I also remember *her* in her pastel pink, bright blue, blazing red petite-sized miniskirted clothing of the era! Short brown hair, brown eyes that could dance with laughter and be somber-serious in reflective thought. I remember *her* those years as I remember *you.*

Now, twenty years later, I laugh through tears at the privilege of holding your hand and telling you something I could not have told you then. You only saw the Poised Professional Adult. I was authentic, honest, but you only saw what I dared to "present." Neither you, nor anyone looking on could know that my secret inner self often sat in my own Job-ashes, weeping on a kitchen table in a silent house, my own heart shuddering with fears of The Unknown.

Anita, you concluded your birthday letter with "Did you ever experience fright in the night . . . or am I the only one . . . *in history?*"

I chuckle again through tears. No, Anita, you are not the only one!! Every searching soul *in history* has experienced fright in the night . . . in the morning . . . at noon . . . in *facing forty*, moving toward aging, toward ultimate mortality. But Forty-Fears are fools! Robert Browning said it best:

Grow old with me.
The best is yet to be,
the last of life,
for which the first was made.

And "the last of life, for which the first was made" grows increasingly longer and more challenging as medical technology increases. In 1928 the average life-span for a woman in America was thirty-seven. In Gail Sheehy's book *New Passages*, she documents that a woman's life, barring accident or cancer, can be ninety-two years. The average lifespan of both sexes is eighty-three years.

Now that you're forty, you have created, with God, the *foundation* for what can be the most productive years of your life. This *first*, on which you now stand, is solid ground for the *last of life*, about which Browning evaluated, "the best is yet to be."

I promise you, my frightened, "helpless quail," Browning was right.

How can I give you such a promise? Because I'm twenty years and six months older than you are, thus, hopefully, twenty years and six months *wiser*. I read your birthday letter, littered as it was with questions. I cannot give you *the answers*, but I can share some things that I have learned in the uniqueness of my own life that may be universal.

As you say of yourself, Anita, in my first four decades, I had competently climbed "my mountain." On its summit, I built My Magical Carousel of Personal and Professional Achievements. Its whirling, spinning music filled the earth, and the carousel horses pranced its rhythms as I sang its lyrics and laughed in its sunshine-pools. Life was *good*!

And then came . . . *Change*.

These last two decades have found me somersaulting upside, downside, upside, downside, upside, downside so often, it could be a Woody Allen movie, except it is *My Life*. My magical carousel burned, and from my mountain I was "hurled into cruel chasms below."

Dear Anita, there is something important I want to tell you today: It was in the "cruel chasms" into which I fell that the great strengths of my life pressed themselves into being. I faced the most challenging moments with a strong sense of self surviving *with God*. I truly believed and dared to prove that with God,

The best is yet to be,
the last of life,
for which the first was made.

The first forty had been golden years. Each day was filled with a radiance so spiced with hidden revelations that my heart sang before each new dawn. Zephaniah had prophesied such years: "The Lord thy God . . . will joy over thee with singing" (3:17, KJV). My Creator companioned me those growing years with His own joy. *Life was joy!* And then came *Change*.

It began in my fortieth year . . . Addison's disease became my diagnosis, as it had been John Fitzgerald Kennedy's, where the adrenals cease to function. The lifeline is daily dosages of cortisone with a mandate of proper rest.

Oh, Anita, I tried, but the hyperactive personality strained against the "proper rest" parameters, and in my forty-first year, I went into adrenal crisis, which is often fatal. The nurses told me I whispered over and over, "I can't ever live like that again!"

Change had come to me. Though unconscious, I knew. I understood. This life-limiting illness was mine. No longer could I deny it.

As the days passed, there came a moment, deep inside, when I heard Jesus' words: "Be of good cheer; it is I, be not afraid."

My inner laughter was shrill at the absurdity as I shouted back, "But I *am* afraid! No, I am terrified! I never knew the fire of a blazing, beloved world could be so devastating! I never knew reality could be so cold! I never knew destruction could be so total! Don't you know? . . . *Life isn't supposed to be like this!*"

Riding on the echo of my sobs were Jesus' words recorded in John 16:33: "These things I have spoken unto you, that in me ye might have peace. In the world ye shall have tribulation: but be of *good cheer*; I have overcome the world" (KJV).

I cried in a limp, broken heap, "No! No good cheer! Not now! I never knew a heart could hurt so much!"

I lay listless as a sawdust doll.

Then with inner ears I heard His compassionate voice: "Christianity is not a guarantee against such knowledge, Ruth. Christianity is a guarantee that *I will be with you* when you face that knowledge . . . and I will bend with you in *redeeming* the situation . . . *if you will allow.*"

I remembered that Katherine Mansfield wrote, "The little boat enters the dark, fearful gulf and our only cry is to escape—'Put me on land again.' But it's useless. . . . The shadowy figure rows on. One ought to sit still and uncover one's eyes."

I uncovered my eyes to look at my "little boat," now rushing through "the dark, fearful gulf" . . . and chose to believe that with God,

> The best is yet to be,
> the last of life,
> for which the first was made.

Anita, mine is a navigator's tale.

> Life hurled me from my Magical Mountain peak
> into an angry, boiling, roaring ocean of *Change*,
> where, in my small boat, my life powered away,
> *far-far-away*, from
> all I had expected . . .
> all I had dreamed . . .
> all I had planned for . . .
> but, Anita, *this is my truth:*
> even when the dearly loved land,
> even when the dearly loved mountain,
> even when the dearly loved carousel,
> even when dearly loved persons
> were lost to me

and the stars were shrouded in mourning
and I throbbed with deep losses
and I was so afraid . . .
oh, so *very afraid* . . .
even then,
even there,
the miracles all around me
would leap to celebrate themselves
and I would celebrate with them,
knowing
even then,
even there,
I was safe
for
even then,
even there,
God was *with me*,
assuring me
the best is yet to be,
the last of life,
for which the first was made.

In that faith, Anita,
I could find the strength
to hoist the sails again,
the will to catch the winds again,
the courage to chart the boat again,
believing an Unseen Hand enveloped
my small hand on the Captain's wheel.

Oh, Anita,
when I was so lost in the raging,
boiling, scalding ocean
of disappointment, of failure,

of rejection, of betrayal,
of loss,
I kept faithful to the trust
that God would guide me to a *New Shore*
that would arise to meet me,
and there,
in that *New Place*,
I would find *new fulfillments*,
new findings, new challenges,
new loves, new promises,
new mountains,
one of which would be *the one*
on whose summit God would enable me
to build a sparkling, spangling, singing,
new carousel!

And, as you know,
He did!

Anita, in your birthday letter, you tell me you are *afraid* of aging
. . . you are *afraid* you don't know *who you are* . . . you are *afraid* of the
unknown future where horror might await. As you heart-share, you
blurt out, *"And when it does come, what is left?"*

Do you remember Medea in the Greek tragedy? Remember the
line of that beautiful play when Medea stands alone, understanding
that everything she cherished in her world is gone, everything is in
ruins . . . and the oracle comes to her where she stands center stage
and says, "Medea, Medea, *what is left?* Everything is destroyed. . . .
Everything is gone. . . . Medea, what is left?"

And Medea responds, *"There is me."*

What do you mean, *what is left* when every human element
known, trusted, loved has been blown to smithereens? What do
you mean, *what is left?*

"There is me."

The dignity, the integrity, the wisdom of those three words has given me an understanding that may answer the burning questions of your birthday letter. Scripture tells us that each of us was divinely hand-stitched in our mother's womb into a one-of-a-kind, never-before-on-earth, never-to-be-again *unique personality*.

The day I pulled out the old Greek drama and those three words jumped out at me, I wrote in my journal,

"There is me!"
What do these three words
mean to me?

I ponder:
God created heaven and earth . . .
and found it *good*.
God created *me* very carefully,
very thoughtfully,
with deliberate design
for specific purpose . . .
and found *me good*.

According to Scripture,
God created *me* in His own image,
imprinting His Spirit in all of my being;
thus something inside of *me*
reaches out beyond *me* always
and seeks to be linked with the stars.

I belong to my Creator
Who made *me*,
Who lives among the stars,
but also
lives deep inside of *me*.

I am important

because
I belong to the Lord!

It is *in God*
that all broken things will be made whole,
that all spirit-wounds will heal,
that all things *lost* will be found.

It is *in God*
that the dense fog of *fear* will lift,
that tears will turn to laughter,
that *all* things will be redeemed,
for nothing is *ir*redeemable.

"There is me."

Let me lift up my head in dignity!
Let me lift up my eyes unto the stars!
Let me reach up to love you, my God,
even as you reach down to love *me*!

Oh! You are the One who created *me*
and brought *me* into being!
You are the One who designed *my person,*
my body,
my mind,
my spirit,
and blessed *me*
with the seal of your goodness,
your love,
your joy,
making *me* a child of your wondrous glory.

In every way, you have made *me*
the offspring of your very being . . .
carefully fashioned in your image.

It is more than I can comprehend, Creator God,
to see *myself*,
to think of *myself*,
to know *myself*,
in this way. . .
and yet, truly,
Scripture assures me
this is *who I am*!

Thank you,
for specifically forming *me* in embryo,
for *growing* me through
all the years of life,
for stretching me and pushing me,
for challenging me and pulling me,
for nudging me and prodding me,
for believing in me and healing me,
for loving me in all seasons.

I fail, I fall, I fear,
but in spite of all my faults,
all my weaknesses,
you continue to grow me
into the new creation I am becoming,
each day, each month, each year, each decade,
as I learn more of *you*, the loving Creator,
and learn more of *my own deepest self*,
whom I must also learn to love,
whom I must also learn to know,
and
I must be willing
to celebrate the wonder of this
God-created precious self.

Yes. The world is a better place

because
There is me!

Anita, it was in the writing of this poem long ago, rereading its truths, trying to *believe* its truths, that I am now able to write you the first poem of the Navigator's Tale, which might be my best answer to your monstrous forty-fears.

This is the bottom line of my response to your fortieth birthday letter: When you accept, in your soul's deepest depths, that *who you are* is God's gift to you, but *who you become* is your gift to God, you can face the future unafraid.

Oh, dear Anita, do consider as your own faith:

Now that you're forty,
the best is yet to be,
the last of life,
for which the first was made.

I love you forever. . .

—Moddy

chapter two

Feeling Out Forty

ANITA HIGMAN

I couldn't bike past the park without taking a moment to play. . . .

It would have all been delightful, except my body didn't go down the tube slide with grace and ease. Fortunately, I managed to scoot free before causing a major kid-pileup behind me.

I couldn't help but wonder if at forty I was acting childlike and spontaneous, or childish and pathetic.

Most of the time, I am trying to fly toward life's bright openings, but I keep getting stuck in the narrow turns of the past. Some things are just harder to scoot free of.

· · · · · ·

DEAR MODDY,

Your response to my fortieth birthday letter arrived today. I read it at the kitchen table in the same spot I had written my fears on that significant night. I was caught by this phrase: "I faced the most challenging moments with a strong sense of self surviving *with God.*"

"Strong sense of self" . . . That is what you were challenging me in this important letter, isn't it? Your exploration of Medea's words brought tears . . . as do all the refrains of Browning's words.

But, Moddy, I have to tell you something: I spend so much time looking back on disappointments in my growing years that I'm afraid at forty I don't really have that "strong sense of self." I don't really believe in the words of the pretty poetry you mentioned.

You see, my past still gets in the way of understanding Browning's words "the best is yet to be." My past still gets in the way of feeling a "strong sense of self." My past still gets in the way of my taking Medea's stance as you define it in your poem.

I know I'm not alone when I tell you I did not have a happy childhood. I was not close to my parents growing up, yet I longed for it. I desperately needed what was divvied up so sparingly . . . affection for Anita. I could write a heavy volume on my past. Instead, I'll just say that I'm carrying the anguish of my loss with me. This baggage gets heavier with each year, not lighter.

Don't you see, Moddy? It clouds my future because I respond to the present while thinking of my past. It's like trying to drive while staring in the rearview mirror. We all know how dangerous that can be. I am bound to crash eventually.

If I let it, the ugliness I felt in my youth can taint what I say, what I do, and how I serve God. It does in the present. It affects my family, my relationships, my "sense of self." Now, of course, it will affect "who I become" in the future!

Oh, Moddy! Could I, at age forty, develop a "strong sense of self," facing all the unknowns with God? You explain it according to God's own Word. My head may accept that, but somehow my heart does not! Sorry . . . I just can't believe it!

You say in your poem, I need to learn more of my loving Creator. But here is the hard part: I need to learn "more of my deepest self whom I must learn to love . . . know . . . celebrate!" Do I love, know, celebrate Anita, the person? Does it make any sense if I tell you that even my professional achievements leave me in an inner mass of confusion? "Who is this wonderful person?"

Well, I really am sane enough to know the answer: Anita Higman

. . . but then, who is she? I'll tell you who she is . . . she is the small child yearning for loving words and affection. Why is this? Was there something wrong with the child? Of course not! I know that truth in my head, understanding all the complexities involved in my home. Really, Moddy, I understand it all . . . it's okay . . . and yet . . . and yet . . .

I know you'd probably say what everybody else says: *Simply let your past go!* But if that were the answer, my troubled youth would be long gone on a train to the next galaxy by now! If I had a dollar for every hour I've talked it all through with myself, I'd be wealthy enough to buy a psychiatric hospital and admit myself. I'm tired of looking at the mess and playing in it. I'd like to clean it up, now that I'm forty!

I look at your words and ponder: "Strong sense of self" created by God as His gift to me, but who I, Anita, become is my gift to God! I can flat-out tell you that sometimes my gift is glorious, but too often it is not!

I'm too immature in my dealings with others. My dream is that people will be attracted to me, find in me fairness, goodness, a sincere smile . . . but the reality is that I'm too often cynical. I think bad thoughts about people, and sometimes I even say them out loud. One minute I care too much about what people think, and then I suddenly treat myself to a release of pent-up resentment for holding my tongue! And then I let out my *real and raw* feelings under the guise of speaking the truth.

Where is the balance? Where do absolute honesty and gentleness sup together? Many times I fail in finding this place of solace. Instead, I'm usually dining alone in a den of squirming irritation and disharmony. For me and my personality, trying to find this place of solace is like searching for an imaginary citadel or a nonexistent utopia!

The truth is, I want to get along with people. Sometimes I do.

Very well indeed. But too many times, I don't. I find that even some Christians are hard to get along with. Is it me? Is it that I'm getting crabbier as I get older? Is this my gift to God?

Oh, Moddy, please help me to find the "strong sense of self" that can move with God, no matter what the future holds! I may not have to pass through all the hardships you have known, but if I do, I want one day to write my own navigator's tale of a divinely hand-stitched Anita with such a "strong sense of self with God" that I can, indeed, become all that God dreamed I could become when He carefully formed the uniqueness of my self, "surviving with Him!"

But now I'm afraid I have to tell you this: The sheer habit of living in the past threatens to entangle me like an addiction. You didn't allow that, but why? How? Was it that you had a perfect childhood in which you knew you were always perfectly loved, so that you easily grew to become a perfect adult?

I know that's a goofy thing to ask! You had a lot of fine things happen to you in your first forty years, but I know you well enough to know that there were sad things too. Nobody really lives a fairy tale.

When I was a collegian, it seemed you lived a perfect life. As you say, I had no clue about the nights you sat in your "Job-ashes, weeping on a kitchen table, [your] heart shuddering with fears of The Unknown." I guess I thought you were always laughing!

I was a kid, Moddy. I only knew fragments. As you only knew fragments of me . . . because you only saw the overachiever whirling about on a college campus. We never took off our masks those years . . . but now that we have found each other in maturity, we speak honestly from our hearts. And that is why these "forty-letters" are so important for me.

So we talked about facing forty . . . but now that you have my response to that letter, tell me more. Tell me how to "feel out forty." Can you give me some magical words? Are there "spiritual laws" here? Did you find a "success formula" early on?

Well, now . . . maybe it's the success formula you told me about in my birthday letter. I need to believe the biblical account of my own creation—to "lift up my head in dignity"—but you say yourself that when you wrote that poem it took lots of rereading to believe it was true! And that was you! It was hard for you to believe it!

Yep, that's how I feel when I reread: It is more than I can comprehend to see Anita, think of Anita, know Anita in this way . . . and yet I do know it's scriptural!

It's easy to read, isn't it? But not so easy to believe. Since it was hard for you to believe this truth for yourself, Moddy, I know it's okay that it's hard for me to believe it's true for me.

Do help me, please. I need you so. . . .

—Your still loving *kid*!

I've Been There

RUTH VAUGHN

Today is my brother Joe's birthday.

He's ten years older than I, and when I called, we celebrated in our typical telephone-teasing way: denying aging, laughing at its reality, sharing anecdotes from our sixty years as siblings. He *always* reminds me that our mother had chosen him to be the diaper helper in that era of washboards. Lyman was too old; Elton was too young; Joe's age was *just right.*

"I did it like the obedient child I was," he reported, "but I told Mother that I would tell you all of your life about my hours of hard work. I never want you to forget. I knew Mother would only remember a sweetly fragrant, adorable baby, but *I was there with the diapers* and I know *the rest of the story.*"

And so it went, story topping story, concluding on the serious note of my gratitude for his being with me physically, emotionally, mentally, spiritually, *through the thickest of the thick and the thinnest of the thin of adult realities.*

"Joe, when my life splattered into a million pieces, you instantly went to work with God to super glue them into the vibrant whole you still believed was possible. You trusted when there was no hope. *'The sky's the limit!'* You shouted the ridiculous phrase at me in your military-colonel assertiveness as if it *were* a possibility." Tears came. "Oh, Joe, how can I thank you for your faith in me?"

His voice was gruff as he laughed. "That's easy! By letting your life today prove how wise I am!"

• • • • • •

MY "STILL LOVING *KID*" . . .

I've read your letter over and over, again understanding every syllable. You're right! It was a goofy thing to ask. I did not have a perfect childhood in which I knew I was always perfectly loved, and I certainly did not grow into a perfect child, nor did I become a re- motely perfect adult! In that sense, I believe we're all "kids" as we look at the lives of other people, including your own life at age forty. Anita, let me tell you: As I observe from age sixty, your life looks pretty perfect from the *outside!*

Let's get to the nitty-gritty of your letter: No! I'm not going to tell you to simply "let your past go." There is nothing simple about such a process. But it is imperative!

Eugene O'Neill said, "None of us can heal the things that life has done to us. They're done before we can realize what's being done, and they then make you do things all of your life until these things are constantly coming between you and what you'd like to be. And in that way, you seem to lose yourself forever."

He capsulizes your last letter, don't you think? He capsulizes my own life at age forty-seven, when I knew I would "lose myself for- ever" unless I made some important *choices.* Life is a series of choices. So my first choice was to do what you said of yourself, Anita. I had to go back to the small girl, living in *that* time, in *that* place, in *that* church, in *that* socioeconomic milieu, in *that* home. I had to take time to understand these elements that had formed my growing-up life.

I *chose* not to lose self. No matter how old we become, the *simple essence of the child* remains. So I put a large picture of the solemn child, Olive Ruth Wood, in front of my computer and began writing por- traits of *that* time, *that* place, *that* church, *that* socioeconomic milieu, *that* home. During this in-depth exploration, I began to understand the *why* of the adult Ruth. As I understood the impact of outside

forces on the growing child, I could "learn to know, to love, to celebrate" the *who* of the adult more clearly.

Such self-knowledge happened only when I *chose* to schedule
hours of time, *chose* the disciplined effort required . . . and the pain,
oh yes! the pain . . . in looking at my past, understanding my past,
accepting my past, forgiving my past, *thus most importantly* understanding myself, accepting myself, *forgiving myself!*

This was my biggie, Anita: I could forgive everyone, everything.
But I refused to *forgive Ruth!* Forgive for *what?* For not being perfect,
as it seemed others demanded. In my lack of perfection, I hated
myself. As you ask, "Was there something wrong with the child"
who later grew to be an adult? Of course not! Yes, my head knew
better, but not my heart! This day I will be my own worst enemy
unless I choose, deliberately *choose*, to learn to know self, love self,
celebrate self! *With all my faults!*

Oh, Anita, there is *NO* perfection in Ruth. Faulty as a flat tire am
I . . . have always been . . . but this is truth: Since childhood, I deeply
yearned to be "pure in heart." In my personal knowledge of that
goal, I find I can *authentically celebrate Ruth even when she is face-flat in failure*
. . . for even there, in the mud, I know I'm trying to love and serve
God, live for Him with a pure heart. *Trying! Trying! Trying!*

I have prayed a lot about how to answer your letter. What sat-
isfies me will not necessarily satisfy you. I cannot give you *the right*
answers, Anita, because I don't know them. I can only share with
you from my life learnings, praying they will stimulate your own
mind until you find answers that satisfy *you.*

I'll begin this way: In my home, I knew love before I had words.
Among the first words I learned to lisp were *"God is love."* Soon my
mother guided me to learn a whole repertoire of Scripture verses,
but two became increasingly significant. When I was five, my
mother took me to her bedroom, set me down, explained God's
plan of salvation. I was "converted" at that age, in that place. After-

ward, Mother impressed on me the need for committing my life to God in all of my growing years. She stressed the imperative of my striving to follow Jesus' simple commands recorded in Scripture: (1) *Learn of Me* (who is Love) and (2) *Follow Me* (in the footsteps of Love).

That same morning, in total sincerity, I prayed the prayer of life commitment and perceived that, even at age five, I *could* understand and be true to those two *simple* commands. As my perceptions deepened, as my life experiences widened, my mother constantly reminded me of those two *simple* commands. She would smile and say, "I never said that learning of God and following Him were *easy*, but the two commands *are* simple."

At age five, I knew that if I chose against learning of God and following in His steps, it was *not* because I did not understand! If I so chose, I could walk the easier road of self-domination . . . but I *could* choose to learn of God and follow in His steps every moment of my life because the commands were *simple enough* to understand. If I so chose, I could walk the more difficult road of God-domination.

I so chose.

I never remember a moment of life when I was not yearning to learn of God and open to following Him, to my best perception. Anita, I made a million errors; I often misinterpreted His guidance; I frequently fell out of His footsteps, but truly . . . those were errors of the head. Before God, I can tell you that from age five, I have consciously tried to be pure in heart! *Tried* . . . note the verb; that was my goal, not my achievement!

When I was sixteen, I was writing a great deal in my journal. I developed my personal lexicon of important terms. It was alphabetical. When I came to *L*, of course, I chose love. I could quote Paul's eloquent definition of love. I reveled in its majesty. But a long-ago day in Bowie, Texas, I wrote, "When I say I love you, I say it with the definition of love being this: I want what is best for you." Seven words. And yet, in all changing seasons of life, Anita, I have done my best to hold true to that succinct, simple definition:

Love is saying, I want what is best for you.

At sixteen, I chose that definition for my love for my parents, for my siblings, for my friends, for the young man I dreamed of marrying, for the children to whom I prayed I would give birth. I wanted to live life with the goal of giving love in that definition to each person in my world: present and future.

As I studied the subject carefully, I became convinced that as I gave love, I would, in the same measure, give freedom to the ones I loved. I perceived that there is no freedom without love and no love without freedom.

Think with me carefully here: Love and freedom are two sides of the same coin, neither fully explorable by a mere mortal, but both of the same essence . . . and both outright gifts from God. And as I tried to follow in Jesus' steps in my growing life, so I would always strive to understand, develop, stretch, those divine gifts.

Let me illustrate from my life. My mother's health broke when I was fifteen, and in a moment of time, I was catapulted from carefree teenager to chief cook and bottle washer for our household. I became responsible for all home duties: meals, washing, ironing, and caring for a bedfast invalid for that first year of her illness. When I was sixteen, one of my brothers became seriously ill, and I became deeply concerned in doing my best for him as well.

In those formative teen years, I determined to accept the full responsibility of *learning* of Jesus and *following in His steps* in every activity of life, to the best of my ability. So I began to understand: Loving requires practice! I knew at age fifteen, at age sixteen, and I gave my full heart to the practice of giving love every day, every way, to my beloved family.

As I matured, I chose to give that same commitment to *all persons in my world.* This demanded that love become a *habit* by *practicing* all that I could see of it in all human relationships. Love is a divine gift, Anita, but I early understood: We must form the habit of *using the gift* in all circumstances by daily, diligent practice, if it is to be effective!

That was my goal in my youth. That is my goal at the age of sixty!

In all the diverse seasons of sixty years of living, I have simply found no way to differentiate between love and freedom. Freedom is the result of love in action. Love is the ultimate goal of freedom. And yet . . . all freedom begins in love. Love frees. I am convinced of this!

In these last decades, I have been lectured as to the *incorrectness* of this view, because many believe this stance denies self-love. This is my answer: What is true for me in the history of my life has been to give, with open hand, love and freedom to each person in my world. So . . . is this not logical? Real love can always give freedom *to* others so each loved one can be free *to* self, *for* self. But . . . just as surely, I believe that real love can always give freedom *to* Ruth, to be my best self *for* Ruth.

Others can choose their best self or their worst self. That is their responsibility. They can choose to love me or hate me. That is their choice.

My only responsibility before God is that I choose *my* best self, and I can still choose to love others even if they do not love me. In moments of rejection, I have said, "You can keep me from your presence; you cannot keep me from loving you." My love for others is *my* choice.

I believe that true love never restricts, never binds. Love always rejoices in growth for others . . . and for self. This is my deliberately, carefully chosen philosophy, Anita: I believe that freedom is not only the result of love in action . . . freedom *is* love in action.

When my most precious carousel burned at age forty-seven,

many close to me found this philosophy foolish, for they observed that I had for a lifetime loved others lavishly, but they felt I had *not* loved Ruth. I pondered *a lot!* During that time, I put up the large photo of the solemn child, Olive Ruth, and went back to her beginnings where *"God is love"* permeated my consciousness before I had words . . . back to my mother's conversation and prayers my fifth year; back to my fifteenth-year challenge to care for my mother; back to my sixteenth year when I wrote in my journal, "Love is saying, I want what is best for you"; back to my forty-first year when Addison's disease grabbed me in all its fierceness; back to all the other challenges of my life.

It was in this careful, long study of Olive Ruth Wood growing that I could reclaim myself. I could know Olive Ruth Wood, love her, celebrate her in the person she had carefully, *deliberately chosen* to *become*.

Anita, think with me: It is my experience that in giving love to others, I find self-love, which frees as truly as love given to another. Is it not true that if I love self *I am free?* Is it not true that when there is self-love, I know that I am free all of my life? *I am free because my reactions to a set of circumstances are never, ever dependent upon the circumstances themselves.* Is that not freedom in self-love as God defines it? I am *not* free if my state of mind is determined by what someone else does to me or leaves undone. *I am not free then.* Another is controlling me. But no matter what another person does to me . . . or leaves undone . . . I can be free so that my state of mind can be filled with love and the freedom to be the best self I can be. *Anita, it is a choice.*

From my earliest decisions, I determined that my state of mind would not be fashioned by what someone else did to me or left undone. I chose to so control my state of mind that, even in painful, suffering circumstances, I would be free to choose to control my mind . . . which would then control my feelings . . . which would then control my behavior . . . and I *could* live daily Jesus' promise of the abundant life.

This I believe: *If I choose* my state of mind, I can be saturated with love and with freedom *in* feelings and *in* behavior. God's love goes right on when our hearts are breaking. God's love has to do with laughter and happiness . . . but it also has to do with tears and loss . . . for God's love is not regulated by our circumstances.

Our awareness can be dampened or heightened by what is currently happening to us, but nothing changes God's love because nothing changes God. God's love is not altered by grief, or injustice, or disappointment, or broken dreams. God's love has to do with inner space, not outer space. Anita, when we *choose* to be saturated with His love inside us, we don't *fear* disturbance from without, for *God is love.*

If I love in this dimension, then, am I not free? Free to understand that my reactions in all diverse seasons of life are determined by *who I am?*

After sixty years of personal life experiences, I believe there are two major factors about human life that determine its quality: (1) What happens. (2) How we *respond* to what happens. We cannot always control what happens. Natural law and the free choice of others set in motion events that affect our lives in areas over which we have no voice.

But topping that factor is this one: Although we cannot control what happens, we *can* completely control how we respond to what happens. And it is this latter factor that is the sure sign *that character is superior to circumstance . . . that faith is greater than fate.*

Our best occupation in this world is not to try to avoid unpleasant circumstances, but to be open to face them with courage that never wavers . . . with faith that saves us from defeat. Years ago I wrote on the flyleaf of my Bible, "The Christian religion is no guarantee against trouble . . . it is a guarantee against defeat!"

We have spoken of Medea when the oracle said, "Everything is destroyed. What is left?" And she answered, *"There is me!"* When everything was destroyed in my life, Anita, I knew I could still *choose* to maintain my dignity; I could *choose* to maintain my integrity; I could *choose* to faithfully love others; I could *choose* to fully love Ruth and determine to be my *best self.*

Anita, mine is a unique history. Yours is a unique history. But whatever that history is, it's gone; it is the past. Oh my child, love it; embrace it. *Rediscover forgiveness.* We can never live life fully until we forgive. Forgiveness comes by *learning forgiveness,* by saying, "It's all right. I still love you."

Your letter reveals your understanding of this. Unless forgiveness is possible, we carry injustices of all kinds on our backs like dead albatrosses, and they *weigh us down.* When we forgive and live in God's love and grace, we can be *free* of those weights, and all of life's energies can be used for growth and beauty. Anita, I challenge you to take the time, the energy, to fully know the *why* of Anita, so you can clearly know the *who.* When that happens . . . and not until that happens . . . you *can* accept the challenge: Never carry your past around like a dead albatross. Let it go. *Learn from it,* and let it go.

Beginning with the diagnosis of Addison's disease my forty-first year when that university carousel burned, I built many new carousels and, with stricken heart, watched them flame in loss too. Someone told me to write a book entitled *Blazing Carousels.* It would be an appropriate title. What I would report in such a book is that after each fire I sat on cold ashes and ultimately could whisper, "Let it go, Ruth. It was beautiful! It was sacred! You loved it! But it *is* past. Release it. Learn from it. *Let it go!"*

I had to understand the complexity of these simple facts: Each of us is a past. Each of us is a future. Who can judge what the future will be? No human guide or prophet can. So we need to focus on the fact that *each of us is a present.* Each of us is a *now* . . . a *now* with a will, a *now* with an intellect, a *now* with desires, a *now* with joy.

Oh, Anita, you at forty, me at sixty, my aunt at ninety . . . we can *become* anything God guides us to be . . . from this point on . . . *anything* that is true to self, honest in God's directed dimension, pure in God-service motivation. The age, the circumstances, are irrelevant for the present *now*, and for the unknown future where we can always find beauty when we know we are *learning of Him*, who is Love, and *following in His steps* of Love. Following the best we know how.

Nikos Kazantzakis says, "You have your brush, you have your colors, *you paint paradise, then in you go* . . . but if you want to paint hell, go ahead and paint it, but then don't blame me and don't blame your parents and don't blame society . . . and for goodness' sake, don't blame God! You take full responsibility for creating your own hell or painting your own paradise." So you see, *it is a choice*!

We're a past? Yes. We're a future? Yes. But this is my belief: The real thing we have to dedicate ourselves to is choosing to follow Jesus the best way we know how *now*! That's where it all matters. But to do that, my child, we have to rid ourselves of words like "never" and "don't" and "can't" and "no" and "impossible" and "hopeless." Delete them from your vocabulary. Remove them from conscious thought.

The greatest dreams accomplished by men and women have been called impossibilities; somebody had to prove the impossible was possible. We can fill our vocabularies with words such as "I will" . . ."I can" . . ."It *is* possible." Why? I'll tell you why, Anita. When I was thirty-three, a diagnostician told me he had no specific diagnosis, but the symptoms that had hospitalized me made him believe serious illness loomed on my horizon. He could give medications to assist in the present, but I had to brace myself for the future.

When he left the room, I astonished myself. With that stark

prognosis, I had assumed I would scream, pull my hair, throw things. Instead, I pulled my Bible from the bedside table and scrawled on its flyleaf, "When Christ dwells in me, the ground on which I stand is holy ground because He is standing on it with me; and because He is a Redeemer God, He will enable me to make creative use of all, even unpleasant, circumstances."

When I wrote that statement of my personal philosophy, I had no idea just *how unpleasant* circumstances could be. Now I think I do. And that faith holds, my dear Anita. *It holds!*

I conclude this lengthy letter of my personal philosophy by asserting that in my sixty years of personal life experience and observing the experiences of others, this is truth:

> *There is no life so lost that it is irretrievable.*
> *There is no situation so broken that it is irreparable.*
> *There is no heart so shattered that it is irredeemable.*
> *He is a Redeemer God!*

I challenge you, "my still loving kid": Prove it out *for yourself.* . . . Make creative use of all, even unpleasant, circumstances. . . . Live Jesus' promise of the abundant life. . . . It is yours *when you choose.* It is a moment-by-moment *choice!*

Know I do love you so. . . .

—Your own Moddy

chapter three

Forty on Fast-Forward

ANITA HIGMAN

An eternity passed while I waited in line. Finally someone barked at me, "Do you have any identification?"

My brain suddenly snapped back into earth mode, and I whipped out my driver's license.

The woman gave me an odd stare and said, "I don't mean to be rude, but are you sure this is yours? The woman on this card is much younger looking."

Astonished, I countered, "Yes, it's me. I'm just pretending to be old today!"

• • • • • •

MODDY,

It's raining today. It's a quiet rain. I almost wish for thunder. The house is so quiet that your last letter leaves me as contemplative as a nun in a convent. This is an unusual role for me. A part of me would rather the thunder crash and Anita rush, dash, be busy "just letting the past go" with a determined flip of my head, but I understand the wisdom of my finally coming to terms with the *why* of Anita. I told you I had spent hours *talking it through* with others. Perhaps it is time to look at the small, oval-faced, dark-eyed Anita and study this unhappy, confused, lonely child and choose to own her, understand her, love her, celebrate her in the unique discoveries that only I, with God, can find.

Moddy, your entire last letter brought me to the feeling of being overwhelmed with *time*. I want to get on with life *now*, yet Anita the woman, Anita the writer, is foundationed in Anita the child. I see the need to make peace with the *why* of Anita so I can move in the way God has in store for the last half of my life . . . in the *who* I become in the next half.

But surely you know my life is already filled to the brim. Do you know how much *time* it takes just to work with my mirrored image? It's frightening! I understand now I will have to face the hard reality that I will never be a goddess. OK, I can hear you chuckling at me. But that is what I have always felt society expected of me. I was to look, dress, and talk like the supermodels on the front of those glossy grocery store mags. In other words, I must be a head-turning goddess or be left behind as a frumpy housemother. The problem is, the older I get, the more difficult it is to keep myself from looking like a gargoyle in the morning, let alone attempting the beauty of a goddess. Of course, when I use that word "goddess," I am referring to the handful of women in the world who were born body-perfect—or at least airbrushed to look that way in ads.

If it weren't for fruit acids, I'd really be a basket case. These new products are helping me take layer after layer off my face. My skin is looking better and people say it looks younger and fresher. At this rate of dead skin removal, I just hope I have some left after fifty!

Moddy, I sit here at my kitchen table, writing to you, sipping my tea, with the rain softly whispering, and my heart races in panic. *Time* is changing me and I don't like it!

Let me tell you of the times I dress up for parties. I get all slicked up with nail polish, rhinestones, and a dazzling dress. I feel princess-pretty upon entering the festivities, but as the music plays and the milling begins, things start happening. I eat my lipstick off with the hors d'oeuvres. My hairdo starts coming unglued, flying up and away, and the perspiration gathers under my armpits. And this all happened *before* age forty!

I'm curious, Moddy, what does sixty feel like? Are you appalled that you have actually grown to such a mature age? Do you wonder where your youth went? Do you look in the mirror in horror that you don't look as you did on our college campus? I mean . . . really . . . is this mirror-reflection thing just going to get worse, in spite of fruit acids?!

This battle with my looks reminds me of my trying to get along with humanity. People start out acting charming (usually) and absolutely wiggly with effervescent friendship expectation. Then some sort of character meltdown happens and sweat bleeds through even the finest intentions. What was once thought to be terribly cute in each other's personality is now driving each other crazy.

I have your letter beside me, Moddy. In reading it over and over, I understand more and more why I find you to be the kindest, gentlest person I know. You learned early how to love and were determined to practice it! You get along with people who don't even want to be gotten along with. You love people who don't even love you.

Well, I *don't* love everybody! Is it really necessary to following Jesus? We're different personalities with different response systems coming from different backgrounds. We aren't ever going to respond to life the same way! You said that your answers are not my answers . . . and yet I do know there *is* all that baggage of my past that needs to be dealt with . . . and that would take *time* . . . and pain. . . .

Do I really need to spend precious time in self-study when I'd rather be writing what I know? Or would I find an inner depth to my whole life personally, in relationships, and in my writing, if I took this kind of disciplined time? But that *would* take me from all the other elements of life that now make me whirl like a merry-go-round! Is that what age does?

I want to stop the world! Hold everything! Time, be still! There are so many things I want to do: play the piano in Carnegie Hall, dazzle children with my juggling skills . . . there is no *time*!

My children think every month drags on like a year . . . yet as I read your weekly letters of your life headlines, I often note your talking about calendar pages hurtling by as if they were caught in an Oklahoma tornado, with birthdays astonishing those coming of ancient age with alarming speed. Do you really say those things seriously, or are you just being silly?

Oh, Moddy, I think that if I swoosh from forty to sixty to eighty as quickly as you seem to believe, I just know I can't get it all done! I don't want to get in a wound-up mode. You well know I have many more dreams for my life that I haven't even begun to fulfill! I can see myself wanting more and more from my life and frantically trying to cram too much in. It's kind of like the talent I have for winding up music boxes too tightly so that they decide never to work again. I don't want to succumb to this temptation in my last decades. I know it will only shortchange my spirit of the lovelier, more holy things in life.

You know, the delight-filled goodies I tend to miss, like morning doves cooing on our lawn, my daughter giggling over her hiccups, the silky brush of iris petals on my cheek. That stuff that makes my shoulders and soul soften when I simply take time to notice . . . but, Moddy, with the quiet moments come guilt! Aren't we all trained from the womb that relaxation and idleness are sins? What is laziness and what is necessary time to rejuvenate? I just don't know!

I remember a favorite quote from Ben Franklin: "Dost thou love life? Then waste not time, for time is the stuff that life is made of."

What is his definition, do you think, of "stuff"? Is it my drive to make all my dreams come true in the next decades? Is it spending more time knowing, loving, celebrating myself? Is it my determination to develop my domestic side—to be the perfect wife, mother, housekeeper, gardener—that fills me with wiggly delight?

Am I not wasting life when I allow times of solitude, self-discovery, just *being*? I'm a dynamo ready to *do*, achieve more and more! You won't think I'm silly if I tell you I want to travel the world and spend a month in the Holy Land! I want to win the Pulitzer Prize for writing great literature! I want one of my plays to be produced on Broadway! I want these things desperately, frantically, and yet I'm dismayed to understand that there is not going to be *time* to develop my talent to that level in all areas and still have time to spend a month in the Holy Land! And no matter how hard I try, I know God may never guide my future time toward Broadway, Pulitzer Prizes, *or* world travel!

Time. Such a tiny word. For the first time, it has enormous significance to me. My life is on fast-forward and I don't like it. I don't like it one bit! But I know I can't change it; I can't buy more time! Even the richest of the rich can't buy more time.

So here I am with your last letter beside me, challenging to go inward when I'm raring to go outward. I'd do both, but there is no time! Moddy, I'm forty. I don't want life to change. I like it just fine the way it is. But Scott and Hillary will grow up and away from me, won't they? Just like your Billy and Ronnie grew to be Bill, the pastor, and Ron, the magazine publisher. Don't you miss them . . . the children laughing in your home? Don't you miss being forty with the big achievements still ahead?

Time changes things. I'm trying to accept the fact.

How will I grow? Who will I become? Is it indeed a choice? Such a hard choice . . . into an unknown future . . . with time rushing like the Indy 500. . . . Well, I don't like it!

Oh, Moddy, I wish you were here to hold me on this rainy day, touch my forty-face and make things all better! But you can't stop the rush of time, can you? Your love can't do that for me. I know that. But your love will gently cuddle me across space. I know that too . . . and in that knowledge, somehow I'm no longer in a panic. But talk to me about *time*. It's an enemy to us all, isn't it? Could it ever be a friend? Help! Tell me you'll still be alive to love me when *I'm* sixty . . . because I'm still going to need you. I won't ever out-grow needing you, my own Moddy. Stay on this earth as long as you can, for I love you so!

—Anita,
with no hope at age forty
of ever being a
"goddess"!

Thanks for the Memories

RUTH VAUGHN

Our home is on the third tee of the Greens Country Club. One of my husband's greatest loves is his backyard. We have "Beauty Spots" of fountains, sculptured trees, flowers, but the centerpiece is a large pool moving 1,900 gallons of water per hour under a small oval bridge into a smaller pool. It is bordered by carefully placed shrubs, flowers, statuary. It is gaspingly beautiful on summer days and is illuminated magic on summer nights.

Today I was working with a basket of flowers on our patio. Not expecting company, I was barefoot, in red shorts and matching T-shirt. To my utter astonishment, my absorption was shattered by the reality of the dusty memory of a wolf whistle, so exciting when I was sixteen! Amazed, I turned to look at the youth who had just stepped from his golf cart. Instantly, his face became as blazingly scarlet as my shorts outfit.

"Oh, ma'am . . . please . . . oh, ma'am . . . oh, please . . . forgive me . . . I . . . oh, ma'am . . . please . . ."

As I began to comprehend what had just occurred, I raced across the small bridge to where he was spluttering his complete humiliation. I grabbed his hand. "Forgive you? Young man, don't you know you have just given an old lady the best compliment of the decade? Of course, your only view was *of the back*, and of course you're disappointed in the age discrepancy so quickly visible in the front, but *you just made my day!*"

He laughed his relief as I confessed, "This is true: I'm sixty . . . didn't ever mean to be . . . but here I am! But thank you for making me feel sixteen again!"

· · · · · ·

Anita, age forty, surely you know you are more delightfully, dazzlingly beautiful *to me* than Julia Roberts *or* Cindy Crawford . . . so let me begin this way:

· · · · · ·

MY FOREVER GLORIOUS GODDESS,

I have your letter in front of me, concluding, "Time is an enemy to us all, isn't it? Could it ever be a friend?"

I believe Robert Browning answered it best (and you've heard it before from me):

Grow old with me.
The best is yet to be,
the last of life,
for which the first was made.

Time can be a friend when it goads us to clearly understand— perhaps on a fortieth birthday—*time is life.* Now, at "half time," its reality allows you to carefully consider and take stock of who you are, where you are in life. It challenges you to be aware of its fluidity, its constant movement, its incessant tick-tock trek to mortality. Stanley Jacobson wrote, "It is a monstrous boulder of an idea to wrap my mind around, the idea of ceasing to exist in this world. And the more I engage the monster, the more confident I am that working to come to terms with finitude is neither morbid nor eccentric but necessary to good mental health."

Of course, he's right. I've proven that, because, as you know, there were seven years when acute physical complications made me keenly aware that death was my constant companion. And I came to know, *death was my friend!*

Oh, Anita, I loved life. I yearned to be present for the mature achievements of my children; I wanted to hold my grandchildren; I wanted to cheer the first American on Mars; I wanted to vote in the election of the first black woman president; I wanted to be a part of *all* the exciting things yet to happen! Leaving earthly life, leaving my children motherless, leaving so many cliffhangers would be sad, but, of course, it was all right. My children were growing solidly into their own identities so they would be fine without me, as would the space program and the political scene. And for me . . . I knew my death would only be a door to the Larger Life where my body would be young, strong, exuberant. In the presence of my Creator.

I don't know what heaven is, of course, but I hope it is not wearing a white robe, walking about barefooted on golden streets, harp in hand. God created the earth and earthly things so eternally enchanting, I hope heaven means "plenty of time" and opportunity to achieve all the things we had neither talent nor time to explore here. I would so enjoy winning the heavenly Olympics in downhill skiing; winning Wimbledon in tennis; being head chef in the heavenly bakery, decorating cakes for at least a millennium! And, Anita, you could play the piano in the heavenly Carnegie Hall there . . . and be the children's chief juggler! Couldn't heaven include those earthy joys? We don't know the specifics, nor do they matter. Heaven will be what God "has prepared." It has to be incredible!

But *until then* . . . let's do "earth-talk." Anita, you stand on the foundation of forty years of life experience with the reasonable expectancy of another forty years of vital, vivid, vibrant life such as the eighty-year-old woman pilot of whom I read recently in a magazine. But it is true, my dear, dear child, you are moving into "the last of life, for which the first was made."

So you can no longer be cavalier with time. It moves swiftly, but I want to tell you this: Time can be your best friend . . . for time is now challenging you to consider *who you are at half time, who you want to become at eighty* . . . what you are doing in the *now-moment*, what you would like to do in your *future years*. My loved Anita, time guides decisions developing the quality of your life now, forever. *Will you take time seriously or just let it slip away? It is your choice.*

And, my dear child, do whatever pleases you with fruit acids and other medical miracles to keep your beautiful face, but ponder what is the good of aging with an unwrinkled face if there's no light behind the eyes, no passion in the voice, no new ideas happening inside your head? I know *that* dreadful image won't happen to you, but it can happen. You know that as well as I. I have friends who are so self-absorbed in body maintenance and image repair, it becomes their one obsession. I beg you, be careful of the temptation of obsession in any area.

Of course, I've *pled* for face-lifts when I've seen my forever-young friends looking much as they did when we were eighteen on a college campus and my mirrored reflection makes me want to pull off the Halloween mask! I'm aging! I was stunned this summer when my grandchild, Ashley, brought her friends to look at my hands, gasping at how *old her hands look*! I study them now and they honestly don't look so bad to me, but at age eleven she found her round, smooth, dimpled hands amazingly different from my skeletal hands, where the network of tiny veins is clearly visible.

Recently, Bob listened to my gasping tale of meeting a woman who had become my friend when we were both eighteen on a college campus. She still looks like the young girl I knew then. *I look sixty!* Ah! The difference! How I yearned for some magician to transform me like some magical wand had transformed my friend. I talked and talked to Bob of the miracle of her youthful appearance, carefully and cosmetically created. I explained the surgeries, the months of recovery, the glorious results. When I was finally silent, Bob said, "Well, I'm sure that's great! But look at the *time* she spent in the achievement. We can put on her epitaph, *She looked forty years younger!*" We laughed.

He studied me a minute. "Is that what you want us to put as your epitaph?" I surprised myself by responding firmly and quickly, "I want my epitaph to read, *She laughed a lot!*" Bob grinned. "Or . . . how about . . . *She lived, loved, and laughed . . . a lot!*"

What do we want on our epitaphs, Anita? That is *the* question, isn't it?

We women do our best to age as gracefully as we can, and our men seem to age with such dignified maturity! *Why?* we ask the Almighty and each other. We look at our handsome men and shout, *Unfair!* but there it is! We can scream about it . . . laugh about it . . . or accept it!!!

For men *and* women, this is true: *Time is life as you choose it to be.* You can deny it or you can seize it, hold it, expand it, shape it to your dreams with God, or it will gallop out of control and disappear. Perhaps *until* forty, it seems for most of us that time is eternal, as Scott and Hillary find it now. Forty can be a "wake-up call" to your opening yourself to discover more of what can *yet be for your life*—in Jesus' promised *abundant life!*

When you were a high-school graduate, you clearly understood the importance of all those choices you would make to form your future. It was the *beginning of becoming.* I believe age forty is a crossroads that can be equally future-determining with equally vital choices to make! You stand on a forty-year foundation. Where do you want to go from here, and who do you want to be as you grow into a *new* beginning of becoming? Life *does* change in the "last of life, for which the first was made."

The Harvard psychologist Ellen Langer says that mindfulness is the key to cherishing life and stretching time. Her definition of the term is to be conscientiously "alert, in control, and open to life's possibilities." Because life events swooshed me off a college campus into a weakened, housebound body, I quickly had to learn a new alertness to the control I still possessed and oh! . . . such an openness to life's possibilities . . . *new* possibilities in a world where I found no collegians laughing in my classes or in my home.

But there, in all that quietness, I wrote my best books, my best stage plays, my best musical books and lyrics, many with my own David McDonald writing magical, musical scores. At SNU, I invited him to collaborate on a children's musical where, as a piano-performance major, he took a drama class to better know how to accept the unexpected opportunity of writing a musical score to my book and lyrics. In those housebound years, he was hired as my professional composer. Two of those musicals have been translated into other languages for ministry. The illness made me "alert, in control, and open to life's possibilities" as nothing else could have challenged me.

The poet Rabelais wrote, "Nothing is so dear and precious as time." In that silent house where I lived for seven years with physical complications dogging my every movement, death close at hand, I understood that poetic line as a most astute evaluation. I had this *time*; I had acute weakness; I had a bright mind. I could choose to give into the weakness or I could *choose* to use all the energies available to use the mind. It was my *choice to make*!

My author friend Paul Maier wrote on the back cover of one my books, "Her greatest creativity and production have taken place after the medical catastrophe." That was true, Anita. Why? I was "mindful" of every life moment. I fell in love with life with more wonder than ever before. I became acutely aware that *time is precious*!

Now I am, again, in vigorous good health, but those seven years housebound, alone with God, with death often holding my hand, makes my every present *today* even more precious. Ellen Langer did experimental studies, proving that "mindfulness" of each life moment improves health, increases brain development, reduces depression, increases self-confidence, lengthens life. She wrote, "Mindful living challenges commitment to *intentional living.*" I think she means knowledge of *time* demands purposeful concentration, prayerful determination to live each day with more *aim* and *awareness of life with God.* Wherever. However. Whatever the changing circumstances.

Anita, long ago you wrote me your response to a specific passage in the book I wrote, sharing my journey through critical illness. It is entitled *My God! My God! Answers to Our Anguished Cries!* If you remember, the chapter you mentioned in your letter began, "Heartbreak . . . I felt the break literally. The crack was so real it seemed to be something I could see. . . . I lay still beneath the covers. . . . Suddenly, I was back in the top of the mulberry tree where I had spent so many hours as a little girl. It was an amazement. How could I ever have been a little girl in a pink ruffled pinafore and careful finger-shaped curls, singing songs or writing poetry in the open arms of the large brown tree?

"But it was true. I could remember the roughness of the bark, the shape of the emerald leaves, the presence of God with me. I caught my breath.

"If God were with me in the mulberry tree, wouldn't He be with me now? There was a sharp intake of breath. My faith was torn up the way a plow tears up a cotton field. Nothing would ever be simple again. . . . My eyes filled with tears as my heart bulged with pleading: *Oh, why don't you explain yourself to me?* In the mulberry tree, it was all so simple. And now I cannot understand. I cannot. I hurt myself with these thoughts because I am not strong enough to think clearly. So I must leave them. I must let them go for now.

"But, God . . . don't leave me. Whatever I find of you in later study . . . for now, *God of the mulberry tree, wait with me. Wait, wait with me.*

"And He did."

In another place in that chapter, I wrote, "I know I may be dead soon . . . but that's not the point. What counts is *right now. I've got this moment, this cupful of beauty."*

Rabelais wrote, "Nothing is so dear and precious as time." When I wrote those words, Anita, I understood Rabelais' line clearly. I knew death was close, thus *dear and precious time made me alert to truth*: I was lying in a beautiful bed in a beautiful home, looking out on soft falling snow, knowing that soon my husband and sons would rush in and love would enfold me. Yes. In that moment, *I owned a cupful of beauty* and I held it carefully as the "dear and precious" thing it was. I was *aware, alert*, grateful!

You wrote, "Time changes things. . . . How will I grow? Who will I become? Is it indeed a choice . . . such a hard choice . . . into an unknown future with time rushing on like the Indy 500?" Yes, Anita, it is a choice, a hard choice . . . into an unknown future, and time rushes on more and more with race-car speed. This is life as I have lived it twenty years longer than you . . . and as I observe my ninety-year-old aunt in her vibrancy. How we handle time is the vital choice!

The conclusion of the book mentioned above may be my best conclusion to your important letter. "The knowledge of *who* by-passes the *why*, and moves on to *how*, which is the *holy ground* upon which the Redeemer God will enable you to make creative use of old-world debris . . . to build a new world.

"This is His answer to our anguished cries. And this answer changes the anguish of 'My God, my God, *why?. . .* ' to the hushed worship of 'My God, my God . . . *you are Redeemer!*' "

I would change these words specifically for you whose world has never exploded into debris as did my whirling university-professor world. Anita, age forty, the knowledge of *who* bypasses *why*, and moves on to *how*, which is the *holy ground* upon which the Redeemer God will enable *you, Anita*, to continue building a beautifully creative life on the solid foundation of forty years . . . and, as God guides, to build new, even more creative worlds in the next forty years.

You weep in the anguish that "time changes things," asking, "My God, *why* does change have to come? *Why* do beautiful, active bodies change? *Why* can't time stand still in this moment with my little children laughing in my home?" My dear Anita, the answer comes in the fact that earthly life is filled with growth, thus change . . . and the comfort is this: God is ever with you in the life changes . . . redeeming, redeeming, redeeming all the losses *into* gains.

I promise.

I promise because I want to share facts I've proven out.

And yes, my beloved child, I'll try to live "long on this earth" in the sheer joy of observing your *becoming the more mature Anita* who will *always* be *my* dark-eyed, dazzling, glorious goddess!

—Moddy

chapter four

A Professional Woman at Forty

ANITA HIGMAN

Fourteen years ago I sat quietly reading a book, not knowing that in a few moments my life would change forever. A whole new direction . . . never to turn back.

I stared at the words on the page, and an idea was suddenly born. I thought for the first time since my childhood, *I really can do this!* In excitement and resolve, I literally screamed it from the bedroom to my husband.

After that, I took my dusty writing dream and decided to make it happen.

With a lot of help from upstairs, I did make it happen.

But at mid-life . . . sometimes even dreams come into question.

· · · · · ·

MODDY, OH MODDY,

Guess what?

I have my own "Erma Bombeck"–type column in a Houston newspaper! Has my photograph . . . the whole works! As your child Ronnie used to say, "Who'd a-thunk it?" Not I! Oh, I dreamed it, but . . . who'd a-thunk it would happen to me? Can you hear my screaming delight in Oklahoma City?

Of course, Peter, Scott, and Hillary celebrated with me and told me how wonderful I am! But now it is night; all are sleeping; and I come with a cup of Earl Grey tea to scribble my Moddy-note of the day's headlines. And I wonder. . .

I wonder if you will give advice to this forty-year-old professional writer. I know you will be honest, if I ask. Well, I'm asking.

Moddy, do you worry about my lack of direction? I have written television scripts, now a newspaper column, books for children, and dramatic plays. So many genres I create. I don't have an agent, so I have to make all the contacts for my works. You know this takes *a lot* of time . . . but I'm also a wife, mother, housekeeper, gardener, daughter, sister, friend, Christian. . . . oh, I'm also the one who handles the wardrobes for my family of four . . . and on it goes!

What do I do? Let's just deal here with the profession! Am I spreading myself so thin that I am not sufficiently focused . . . or am I simply diversified to maximize success in this field? Writing is indeed the intoxicating joy I thought it would be, yet I want more! Am I expecting too much of myself?

I want what God desires of me in my writing, Moddy, but sometimes I don't hear from Him. If only God would write things on the wall as He did once in biblical times, I would follow His will to the letter. I just don't know what He has in mind for me.

Oh! It would be so much easier to follow Him and live His promise of the abundant life, if He would talk to me somehow. Moddy, I've got it: He could write on my bathroom mirror in the morning. Something like, "Anita, I want you to start writing a children's picture book about elephants this morning. I am most fond of elephants. Later today you should call your friend Melissa. As a mom with four children, she needs encouragement. And don't forget to clean house, because your aunt Harriet is making a surprise visit in two days."

Do you see how easy life would be if God would only give me

specific direction? No confusion. No messy house. All well in my world.

But . . . not only is my mirror clear of godly messages in the morning, sometimes my prayers seem to come back empty too. You admit you have misunderstood God's leadings—"fallen face-flat in failure"—so I guess you know what I'm talking about here. But as you get older, do your prayers come back with clearer answers than before? I'd really like to know.

Now to another concern: Recently I took a writing job outside my home for a couple of weeks. I was amazed at how young my co-workers were . . . and how old I was in comparison! I decided it takes grace to allow a woman twenty years my junior to be *my boss*! Most interesting experience . . . but there was something else that worried me as I observed: America *dotes* on the young!

I had thought there was a natural built-in age-related pecking order . . . I mean, by the very nature of the letters we are writing just now, there is a hierarchy of wisdom related to age. Right? And when I'm sixty, I hope that I, too, will have gained a certain amount of respect because I have lived so long and hopefully absorbed valuable knowledge of life along the way. It would be fun to write wise "Anita responses" to some forty-year-old youngster when I am a sage sixty! It could happen! That would be as delicious as my newspaper column!

But, Moddy, I don't find respect for aged wisdom in the workplace. Mature, skilled, wise professionals are often "retired early" or simply let go to give room for some young whippersnapper to take over! I see people changing careers at fifty or sixty because they have no choice in the matter. I find that grossly unfair, but I guess it's another fact of life that we must swallow, or become embittered.

That leads me to another area I wanted to discuss: starting a new profession because one *chooses* to do so! I keep hearing people I know talk about their career frustrations. Some of them even quit and start something new. Moddy, why did we do this whole college thing if so many of us change our minds after a while and begin again?

That question is hard for me to ask you because you are a former college professor. And . . . you were *my* college professor once upon a time. But this question still intrigues me. *Why* do so many people seem to know in their heart of hearts their life's calling, spend years getting ready for it, and then burn out after about ten years? Is it a natural life cycle everyone goes through? Or are there some personalities simply less likely to remain committed to one career throughout a lifetime? Do you think it's linked to a selfish panic within a mid-life crisis? Or has society made this problem up because it has a need to pigeonhole everything? Is it a "recalling" of professions like the recalling of defective cars? If so, does that mean God changes His mind? Or is it a fresh and wondrous and holy thing to have two or three careers in a lifetime? Perhaps you recommend it highly! I'd like to know.

For me, I can't imagine myself wanting to give up writing for a career in *anything else*! I just have a *need* to write!

Do those people who make career changes hunt the changes down and invite the inevitable in, or does it more often come as a total shock that engulfs them unwillingly? The last possibility bothers me—that they could have their lives so changed that what they adore now will mean nothing to them someday. What a frightening thought.

Moddy, did you always know you would be a writer? Did God "call" you to write, or was it more of a natural knowing that this was what you could do best? In all the years of your life, no matter what happened, have you always wanted to write? Will you want to write even at the end of your life? I mean, is writing that important to you?

Talk to me, please. I know I've hit you with a mother lode of questions . . . but I dare to write all this hurry-worry-flurry because I really do respect your philosophies. And, Moddy, it is not simply because you have been alive longer than I have . . . it is more because of how you have handled the years of your life! Do you know how many countless people you have inspired? I happen to know there are a lot. And I'll tell you something else: You are my personal *hero*!

This is another strange kind of letter, but this is how I feel tonight and I knew you'd want to know. So here it is! I'll put it in an envelope and mail it to you tomorrow . . . and when you receive it, promise you'll feel my enduring love. . . .

—Anita Higman,
Herr Professional!

Who Do You Want to Become?

RUTH VAUGHN

Between the years 1984 and 1992, most of my time was spent in traveling around the United States and Canada doing public speaking engagements at conventions, seminars, retreats, and many creative-writing workshops. Although I signed autographs whenever and wherever asked, I always formatted a specific time following each event in which I would sit at a table and write in the books of those who chose to take the time to stand in line and wait.

One night a young woman gave me a book, and when I asked her name, she told me this was her second creative-writing workshop under my lectures, and in the last hour, she had determined to change careers. Although pressed for time, I sincerely promised her that I would remember her and pray for her in the challenge of finding the fulfillment of her lifetime dream: working with words. I was true to my word, as was she.

Within the year she wrote to tell me she had given up her well-paying job in a computer company and accepted a less lucrative job with a small magazine. I wrote my joy in reading of her happiness in her new job. That was nine years ago. *I went to the mail today and found an envelope on which she had printed: YOU WON'T BELIEVE GOD!* I tore it open and my eyes sped through the news that she had grown through the ranks in the magazine and was now officially its editor. This promotion was unexpected. Her letter was rhapsodic, as was its reader discoing in my circular drive.

Sandy took the big dare to make a major change in her income, in her lifestyle, in every facet of her life. In letters, I know the story well. She ate lots of stew, wore the same coat for years, and rarely went to the symphony. Now she had achieved in a dimension she had previously not even dared to touch.

At mid-life . . . sometimes impossible dreams do come true!

· · · · · ·

ANITA HIGMAN, HERR PROFESSIONAL, MAY I SALUTE YOU?

Of course, I heard your scream in Oklahoma City, and surely you heard me scream my joy when I read the news and displayed your very first newspaper column to Bob! I clapped my hands, danced about, sang with Peter, Scotty, and Hilly, "How awesomely amazing is Anita!"

Bob grinned in shared happiness in your achievement . . . and laughed in all the appropriate places at your inimitable column! Only Anita! How incredible you are!

So you want to ask me some professional questions. I'm honored.

Let's handle them in the order they appear in the letter beside my computer. The first: "Do you worry about my lack of direction?" My answer: No. Then you ask, "Am I expecting too much of myself?" No. You ask the really tough one about when I pray, do I hear God more clearly with advancing age? I honestly do not think I do. About career changes made by deliberate choice, you wonder if I recommend them highly? Here the answer changes: Yes, oh yes . . . if indeed it is *true to that unique self in that unique time of life.*

Jonathan Swift wrote, "Although men are accused of not knowing their own weakness, yet perhaps few know their own strengths. It is in men as in soils, where sometimes there is a vein of gold, which the owner knows not of."

This is true for us all, Anita, but truer for some than others. One of my friends became a doctor because his father had been a doctor. It was a given that he would be a doctor as well. And so it was.

But at age forty, during a soul-searching time, he admitted he hated the frantic pace, the life-and-death responsibilities. As he pondered his *whys*, he began to know that what had been true for his father was not true for him. He had always been a bookworm. At parties, when asked, "What would you do with your life if you could do anything that would please you the most?" Instead of laughing with the others, saying, "I would win the lottery and lie on sun-drenched beaches" . . . he would always respond seriously, "I would fulfill my childhood dream of owning a bookstore."

A bookstore, indeed! The dream was absurd! Everyone said so!

With one exception: his wife, an RN, who understood her husband better than others. At forty, Anita, they began preparations for a career change, a life change.

When the last child graduated from high school, the family took the great dare. The children agreed to work for college expenses. The parents took their entire life savings and purchased a bookstore. They both continued to work part time in their medical professions, juggling hours to handle the bookstore. After a few years, she was able to go back full time to the profession she loved while he gave full time to fulfilling his childhood dream of the profession most *true* to the uniqueness of his God-created self: managing a bookstore.

Anita, I must encourage you to read sociologist Gail Sheehy's monumental book *Passages*, in which she documents an almost universal fact that every seven years there comes some unusual movement in a person's life. I had heard it; I didn't believe it, until I read her book and was astounded to study my life, discovering it was true! I studied my life history and could scribble in the back of the book that in some significant way, something in my life has honestly changed each seven or eight years! I was amazed!

In this book, she has a "must read" chapter entitled "The Age Forty Crucible." This will be of assistance to you personally and give you a greater understanding of your friends who find frustration in the careers for which they had prepared. I also recommend that you read her new book, *New Passages*. Since *Passages* was published in 1976, she finds a New World has developed. She asks the reader to consider:

> . . . 40-year-old women are just getting around to pregnancy.
> . . . 50-year-old men are forced into early retirement.
> . . . 55-year-old women can have egg donor babies.
> . . . 65-year-old women start professional degrees.
> . . . 70-year-old men reverse aging by twenty years (with human growth hormone).
> . . . 80-year-olds run marathons.
> . . . 90-year-olds remarry and still enjoy sex.
> . . . And every day the *Today* show's Willard Scott says, "Happy Birthday!" to more 100-year-old women.

But that's another book for another time. *Passages* can give you insight into life growing into forty and even to sixty-five, but her major focus is *where you are now and how you got that way.*

In my childhood, the theology of preachers to whom I listened, including my own father, was, "God has a blueprint for your life at conception. Follow it and you will always be happy." To me, that meant there was one plan that would give me one road, one expected life role. *That is a wrong concept!*

As I have lived, I've been incredulous to understand that the word "blueprint" is too static for the dynamics of a Creator God who gives *free choice to each child.* As you look at my life, Anita, you find natural law, the choices of others, new opportunities, and new self-discoveries have forced me to walk new, unexpected roads, learn new, unexpected life roles, accept new, unexpected, increasingly difficult challenges. And God has been with me. When beloved roads dead-ended . . . when the curtain closed on familiar life roles, when everything planned for was denied . . . the Redeemer went to work to make *creative use* of all that was lost.

Carl Jung wrote, "We cannot live the afternoon of life according to the program of life's morning—for what was great in the morning will be little at evening, and what in the morning was true will at evening have become a lie." At sixty, I understand his words.

Those are my "quick answers" to your "mother lode" of questions in your last letter. Now let's deal with the most pressing discussion in your life.

Anita, the reason I do not worry at the diversity of your writing genre is because it is only in the writing of *differences* that you can discover your major love! I believe it's only when you put your mind to diversity, you come to know what is true and honest for the uniqueness of Anita, as God dreams of your life's personal fulfillment since He created it. You're not expecting "too much" because you are open to finding His perfect guidance.

As you stand on the threshold of the decades following forty, you are beginning to perceive more clearly the reality of time. In my life, of course, events hurtled me out of the known into the unknown very soon after my fortieth birthday. But if your happy achieving life remains wide open on a smooth highway where you can reach for any goal, ultimately you will need to *choose specifics.*

In your earlier letter, you spoke of wanting to win the Pulitzer Prize for great literature and write stunning hits for Broadway. I know you were just reeling out dream stuff. That's great—as dream stuff.

The reality is, I don't know of anyone in history who won the Pulitzer Prize for great literature *and* wrote stunning hits for Broadway! I've read all of Annie Dillard's books, one of which won the Pulitzer Prize, but I find no indication that she would have the skill to write the drama books *you* have written! On the other hand, Neil Simon's Broadway hits thrill all of us as we watch them on television, in the movies, or in local productions. To my knowledge, Neil Simon would have no interest in writing *your* expository works, hoping for the Pulitzer Prize.

But I could be wrong! Annie Dillard may dream of writing a Broadway play and Neil Simon may dream of writing serious exposition . . . but both of them would know those dreams could never come true for them. Why? TIME!

Anita, you have to *choose*! If you honestly *want* to write a play to be staged on Broadway, you will have to make drama the major focus of your work. If you find you want to write exposition like Erma Bombeck, you will have to make that style of writing your priority. At age forty, you are still exploring the terrain. I believe this is imperative now, but ultimately, you will have to pick and choose. In this lifetime, *you cannot have it all* in professional accolades.

Also there is this: Gail Sheehy reports that among 1,500 achievers randomly selected from several editions of *Who's Who of American Women*, slightly more than half have married. But first, once they had their degrees, they devoted an average of seven years' undivided attention to their careers. But note the number who chose career over marriage for all of their lives.

Helen Gurley Brown wrote a book entitled *You Can Have It All*, but she was wrong. Although she handled a successful career and marriage, she deliberately chose to have no children. She does know you *can't* have it all! Annie Dillard won the Pulitzer Prize, but she states she deliberately chose against marriage because writing was her first love! Each person needs to confront the reality of TIME!

Of course, you chose as the priority of your life marriage and motherhood, with your professional goals in secondary position. I believe, Anita, the panic you feel now—while time is breathing hotly on your neck, pursuing you as *your enemy*—comes from your feeling cheated that you can't have it all. There just is not *time*!

Time is *your friend* only if you take careful consideration of what you really want to do with it. Where are your priorities? Home over career? Being over doing? Self-knowledge over success? Of course, you can have both, but too often I observe women choosing career over home. Doing over being. Success over self-knowledge.

It can be so easy. You wrote recently that under the demands of a writing job outside the home, you became aware that your children might be looking at the black-haired woman absorbed at the computer, wondering, *Who is she?* I hurt with you in the dilemma. You love your work; you love your children . . . but surely under time pressures of the career, the children will *stay* children . . . until *you* find time to be their mommy? It won't happen. You know that! And you panic, shrieking for God to write His specifics on your mirror and *then* you would know what to do when. Don't count on the writing on the mirror, Anita.

"Be still, and know that I am God" is a commandment, in my view, as much as the famous ten recorded in Exodus. And it is much harder to obey!

Anita, you know this is truth: It is only when you schedule your regular life to have time alone with God that you are most likely to find His perfect guidance. It comes in quiet openness—in *time-blocks*—in His presence.

Dear Anita, I grew up in the world of the clergy. I know ministers who rush through a demanding parish world who *never* schedule time for quietness with God. Even as God's representative on earth, they role-play. Why? They do not make the disciplined decision to constantly fill and refill their souls with God's presence. If that is true of clergy, of course, it is true of others.

One of my friends who has been a Christian "since birth" can quote whole chapters of the Bible verbatim with breathtaking accuracy. He administrates a large hospital. It is a demanding job, at which he works sixteen- to twenty-hour days, seven days a week. In the beginning, he told me he prayed on the run and that was enough. He would say, "I'd like to schedule church and prayer times, really I would, but I'm just *too busy for set times!*"

This man is now in his fifties. The last time we were together he spoke of his broken marriage, the alienation of his children whom he never took the time to know, and his great career success with a heavy sadness: "Were I given just one more day to live, I would go on with my routine duties! I would have nowhere else to go, nothing else to do. I have made my career my life." He gave a small, sad smile. "On my epitaph, they'll write that I worked long hours every day."

Such an epitaph was not his life's goal. He did not consider the life consequences with time ever pushing his life forward, until it became too late. He intended to make memories with his wife, friends with his children, but he postponed it until it was no longer possible to do these things. His wife and children live other places now, with other lives. He knows me, a casual friend, better than he knows those whom he loves the most. *Time!*

You asked about my professional life. I have no memory of the time before I could read or print in a Red Chief tablet with a stubby pencil. My mother had been a schoolteacher; my father was a minister. I was born to parents in love with words. I wrote because I had to! In my world, I never considered that I would write professionally. So far as I knew, published writers came straight from heaven. They did not grow in small parishes.

God had other plans. To my astonishment, the doors opened: when I was twenty-one my first magazine article was published; when I was twenty-two, my first book was published. By twenty-three, I was writing everything—not only magazine articles and books, but Sunday school curriculum for two-year-olds through Golden Agers. I wrote Vacation Bible School curriculum for every age; I wrote television scripts and screenplays; I published drama of every type from skits to three-act plays, even the big musicals for which I wrote book and lyrics, and yes, my own newspaper column!

But when I went to Southern Nazarene University to teach, I knew I had to choose. As difficult as it was, I cut all of my writing to one stage play and one book a year.

Like you, Anita, I was born with a "need to write." Not necessarily professionally . . . that came about in God's serendipitous guidance. But words are my oxygen. When I am hospitalized, I beg for tablet and pen. Even with tubes coming out of me everywhere, I always manage to scribble my tumbling thoughts in spidery scrawl; later, I spend time developing them when I am home with strength and a computer! Writing has nothing to do with my profession; pouring out my heart on paper is how God created me. Yes, I would like to write until the very end of my life!

From 1983 to 1994, I published nothing. That was a period too private to share publicly. Still I wrote. Constantly I wrote: journals for myself and one-to-one books to my family and close friends. I prayed I would never publish again. In that period, I took time to survey life's territory both before and behind me. It was during this time that I took the time to study Olive Ruth Wood carefully—to understand her *whys* and learn to understand, love, celebrate her *who*.

I was no longer Ruth, the writer. I was Ruth, the person! In many ways, it was the most important period of my life. Gail Sheehy wrote that at some point "most women pause to reconsider both the inner and the outer aspects of their lives and then try to rebalance whatever distortions they feel between personal contentment and worldly aspirations." This was true for me.

In my life, as you know, I am publishing again and hope to do so until I'm ninety-two! But I only write books. I enjoyed drama, but

I know now that I never want to write a stage play again. *You* write them, and let me applaud!

And if my physical strength fails for any professional projects, I will continue to write for myself and those I love. If my fingers or eyesight make this impossible, I'll try to adjust to putting my beloved words on a tape recorder, although I dislike that intensely! I think through my fingers! That is who I am!

You are more like me than most. As you know, Bob speaks only in bottom lines. He would not, indeed *could not*, write a book at gunpoint. *Anything mechanical* is what is true for the man I love. It is the *difference* uniquely God-created in each of us that we cherish. I'll never understand his motors; he'll never understand my books, but we *understand each other*!

Who are you, Anita, as a professional woman, age forty? Who do you want to become in the next decades? When you can fully answer the first question, you will know how to consider the second. You may be stunningly surprised at what you discover as you prayerfully, carefully consider this challenge:

> *Grow old with God.*
> *The best is yet to be,*
> *the last of life,*
> *for which the first was made.*

My dear child, thank you for inviting me for discussion. Only *you* can find your way with God in the last decades for which the first were made. Know that my prayers enfold you without ceasing. . . .

—Your own Moddy

A Sexual Woman at Forty

ANITA HIGMAN

"Yes, I'd like to buy that lacy red negligee," I told the clerk as discreetly as I could without muffling the words. "It's really just *perfect*. It's for my honeymoon."

The woman smirked. "Sure, honey." She yelled to the man in the back. "Hey, Al. This lady wants the Red Hot Special. That's the last one in the window, so just strip down the mannequin and then give this lady a 5 percent discount."

I turned redder than the nightgown in the window and edged toward the door. "That's OK. Maybe my honeymoon doesn't have to be THAT perfect."

• • • • • •

MY DEAR MODDY,

Wow, do I have a topic today!

Sex.

It's the subject everybody thinks about, and nobody wants to answer questions about. Am I right? (I already know the answer to that question.)

I hope you don't mind visiting with me about this untouchable subject. You are such an open and compassionate person, I feel sure you'll welcome my questions.

As you know, Peter and I have been married almost eighteen years. We love each other very much, and our understanding and love for each other has most definitely grown over the years.

BUT . . . in the physical realm of matrimony, if we were to be rated on a scale of one to ten on our "joy in sex," we'd score about a three or a four. That part of our married lives runs like a flat tire. In other words, it has a tendency to fall into ruts and flop a lot.

Unfortunately, I got some rather confusing information in that area growing up. When it came to sex, my family reacted like many did at that time, by simply ignoring the topic. We didn't even use the words "sex," "pregnant," or "period." Menstrual cycles were called a time to be "sick," pregnancy was "in the family way," and sex was presented more or less as a painful duty.

When *the* sex "talk" was presented to me, parent and child weren't even in the same room! By the time we had finished our "talk," I was so scared and aggravated by the whole thing, I determined right then and there I would never marry. After that one time, sex was rarely ever brought up again in our family.

Because I wanted and needed real information, I went to a book about sex. This turned out to be a disaster because the book was not written from a Christian perspective and the information I received was frightening and crude.

But what could I do? No one else wanted to talk about it. I went searching out of sheer frustration. I wish there had been honest communication between my parents and me. I wish I had found wholesome materials to read on the subject. Isn't that the way He would want it to be? After all, it was God who created sex in the first place! Right?

When I occasionally get squeamish about this topic, even today, I remember a book in the Bible called the Song of Solomon. It is very graphic in its wording, as you know. I remember reading that book when I was a kid. I absolutely could *not* believe it was in the Bible.

But it is.

And for a reason. I have heard it is merely symbolism, but God could have used many other word pictures besides the erotic desire between a man and a woman. He chose, however, to express what He had to say in that way. Sometimes this still surprises me about God!

Later in life, I got the general impression from books and movies that sex should be out-of-this-galaxy glorious, so I was now at least awaiting glory instead of misery.

But after years of gathering a hodgepodge of sexual information, I arrived at my wedding night with some silly notions and perhaps too much expectation. I had, of course, spent zillions of hours fantasizing about how spectacular *that* moment would be.

I reeled with nervous excitement while we carried our luggage to our honeymoon suite, fearing that I would surely be kidnapped before the actual "event." I wasn't, of course.

Once secured in our honeymoon haven, I nervously changed into three different sensuous outfits. Finally, with the perfect one on, I made my formal entrance down the long staircase in the honeymoon suite to my awaiting Prince Charming. Just like in the movies!

Somewhere in that perfection, my Prince Charming decided to close the drapes. But they wouldn't close, so we had to sneak around in the dark all night for fear of anyone seeing us in our splendor. We should have called room service, but alas, we were amateurs at honeymooning!

Anyway, while stumbling around in the dark, I decided to make us a romantic bath with lots and lots of candles, which I had painstakingly packed in our suitcases. With the candles aglow and the stage set, we suddenly and maddeningly became all arms and legs in the tiny bathtub. How come it never happens in the movies that way?

Anyway, after the suds were dried, the eternal wait was over. It was time.

Something happened, Moddy. And wonderful wasn't a part of it. I found the process of making love to be very painful. Everything was rushed and clumsy, with very little sensitivity.

All at once, the mood changed. Coldness and frustration seeped into bed with us. Suddenly, I didn't feel sexy anymore. I felt like a failure. We both turned over and went to sleep. My heart nearly broke that night. My dreams of the perfect first night simply didn't happen!

The patience. The gentleness. The romance. The ecstasy never came. Some emotional and even spiritual part of me *died* on our honeymoon. And after eighteen years of marriage, we have never fully recovered from that trauma.

In the beginning of our marriage, we were afraid I'd get pregnant, so we had to be careful. Then, when I couldn't become pregnant, science replaced the sensual and sex evolved into a machinelike precision ritual.

After I finally conceived, I had a miscarriage. When I was pregnant a second time, we were afraid to have sex because of the miscarriage. Now, of course, we are afraid of my getting pregnant again in my fourth decade, especially after two C-sections, two miscarriages, and nearly losing my two children in dangerously premature labor and heavy bleeding episodes.

As far as I know, sex is scintillating only in movies and books. That's just my personal experience and opinion.

Moddy, I don't think we'll feel totally safe until menopause is over. I just hope by then I'm not too tired to have sex!

But now it seems that every time we try to move in the desired erotic direction, the kids burst in with games and giggling and vital news about the pet salamander! This is true!

And the kids are only a part of it, Moddy. This is also true: Sex is just so hard to schedule into our schedules right now! I know the movies ignore such things, but we are responsible people! Even if there were a roaring passion fire to tend, there are too many hydrants gushing water until even the smoke is a memory! This is serious. With jobs and kids and school activities and careers and household chores and grocery buying and meal preparation and dirty laundry and yard work and church functions and on and on—where is there a moment anyway?

As the years have gone by, we have tried and we have improved, but we both dream that sex surely was meant to be so much more than what we are experiencing.

If you don't want to answer this letter, I'll understand. I promise. Act like you never received it if that's more comfortable for you. But since I know I can tell you anything, I'm going to dare to give you this confession. If you do want to respond to this letter, I'd really like to know if we can expect to ever see better days in this area of sex. I wonder if other people have had bad starts as well and then recovered. We love each other, and I would like sex to be *wonderful in reality rather than in fiction*. Do you think there is hope, Moddy? Can *the magic* still happen for us?

> —Love from your Anita,
> who is wondering why
> the birds and bees are
> still circling!!

P.S. I do remember a wedding in the Bible where a miracle from Jesus enabled the bride to serve the best wine at the last of the party. In intimacy and lovemaking, I would like to become romantic Cinderella giving the "best wine" as my marriage offering to my Peter, who is still my beloved Prince Charming! Fairy-tale sexual fulfillment can happen in real life, can't it, Moddy? I hope you don't mind my asking!

You're Never Too Old!

RUTH VAUGHN

Today an early morning phone call set the entire schedule off balance. Bob likes everything on *his* time. So we swooshed through all the morning duties, and he finally turned to me with a frown. "You know I'm going to be late to work!"

"Such a sad story!" I teased, since it can be no big deal considering he owns the company.

He frowned. "You *know* I don't like to be late!"

He rushed down the hall with papers in hand, then realized he hadn't kissed me. He ran back, grabbed me . . . *And then it happened!* Instead of the quick peck customary in these circumstances, he held me Rudolph Valentino–style and gave me a long, lingering kiss that left me breathless in his arms. Seeing the shock on my face, he laughed at his own unexpected action.

And then—I could not believe it!—my dignified husband whirled me from the kitchen, through the fireplace room, and into the piano room as we awkwardly danced, while he sang from some dusty memory corner Tiny Tim's "Tiptoe Through the Tulips."

We finished with a big flourish and fell in a heap on the floor, laughing, giggling, with soft kisses like teenagers. *And then it was over.* . . . We got up, brushed ourselves off, Bob grabbed his papers from the kitchen table and rushed to the car. And I . . . I stood in the driveway, waving, blowing kisses, and thanking God *true love remains electrically exciting even when a couple is sixty-three and sixty.*

It ain't the age! It's the open, vulnerable sharing!

• • • • • •

MY BEAUTIFUL CINDERELLA . . . YES! YES!

Not only do I want to talk to you about this vitally important part of your life, I want to say in one word: "Yes!" Fairy-tale sexual fulfillment can come true for you! A sexual woman at forty and in all the years to come can be the "best wine"!

I can tell you that, my child, because I'm sixty and know my sexual fulfillment with Bob.

And then there are my parents.

They married in *the* Puritan era. My father had never touched my mother, much less kissed her. He was pastoring in Oklahoma. His wife had died in a "flu scourge" along with a new infant boy. As a dynamic preacher, he was often asked to come back to Erath County, where he was born, to preach for the annual "camp meeting" in a brush arbor where people camped on the grounds in tents and cooked over open fires.

My mother was an "old-maid" schoolteacher. It was her *choice*. She told me and my friends all of our lives, "I knew I would never marry unless a prince came along!" We were enchanted, privately vowing to wait for our "prince"!

Back to the story: My mother played the piano for every camp meeting, so my father was acquainted with my mother, aware of that beautiful, dark-eyed, small face, her magical fingers on piano keys. He lived alone in a parsonage with four daughters, until his oldest daughter married and left home. He began writing to my mother; she wrote back. She kept all her love letters, bound them with blue ribbon, and gave them to me when I was sixteen. I found so much poetic idealism in my mother's letters that I understood more clearly my parents' stories of her total ignorance of sex and how babies were made.

They married in Texas, where she lived, and then boarded the train back to Oklahoma. It was a few hours before he had the courage to put his arm about her. Instantly, she drew herself up, exclaiming, "Please remove your arm!" This is a true story. I have listened as both my parents recounted it, shockingly absurd even in my youth!

Daddy didn't say anything. When they were finally alone in their bedroom on their wedding night, they sat together on the bed. Mother declares she thought those moments would only be for rejoicing in the wonder of their finally being married, with the glory of spending the rest of their lives together. She had no faint glimmer of *anything* physical! My father believes it!

When he finally put his arms about her, kissing her, she pulled back in gaping astonishment. "Why are you doing this . . . now?" Equally astonished, my father explained that this was the beginning of something beautiful that married people do. Totally bewildered, she said, "But . . . I thought that only happened when you were wanting to have a baby . . . and something happened one time. . . ." Her voice trailed off and my father suggested they go to bed and sleep. The subject was shelved for their wedding night.

I remember one time, my senior year in high school, when my mother and I sat on the back porch while my father was washing the car in the driveway beside it. He began telling this tale in such dramatic fashion that both Mother and I laughed until we cried. It was so funny *then*! It was not funny when they were in the dilemma.

The day after the wedding, my father suggested that my mother get back on the train to Texas and talk with her mother about the "facts of life." Not one syllable from anyone had ever been shared with my mother about *real life*. Anita, this is true: She would conclude some of her love letters to Daddy, "We will hold hands all our lives and go into the sunset together!" That is all she knew about marriage!

When my mother returned to Texas, my grandmother refused to talk to her about the private subject in any helpful way. Instead, she gave full vent to her rage against my grandfather, who "had his way with her" whenever he pleased, making babies whenever it happened! She, the woman, had no control over *anything*!

My grandmother's release of her bitterness against the sexual part of her marriage confused and terrified my mother, for she had considered her father the kindest, gentlest, most tender man in the world. Mother grew up in a happy home, for of course her mother kept secret her resentment while the children were young. My grandmother had understood early on that her only option in life was to marry a man, keep his house, and have his babies, with no thought of her own emotions, dreams, or plans. Everything was pressed down inside as her husband controlled her destiny.

My grandmother's frank resentment sent my mother back to my father as ignorant as ever of exactly what was expected of her . . . and filled with monstrous fears and trembling terrors. Before her marriage to my father, she had chosen to defy tradition in her generation. She knew many sneered that she was an "old maid." Mother didn't care. Until a *prince* came along, she had chosen to live her life as an independent career woman: teaching school, playing the piano for church and all community functions. She lived alone, in control of her own emotions, her own dreams, her own plans. Was my father going to destroy her? She had been called "Miss Nora." Now she would be known as "Mrs. Wood," but she hadn't thought that the essence of "Miss Nora" would be consumed. By marrying this handsome, eloquent young preacher, she had found her "prince." But would he imprison her instead of simply "holding her hand into the sunset"? Obviously, marriage involved more than "holding hands"!

When my father heard her report from the Texas trip, he kissed the top of her head, told her not to worry, and went away. He returned with a book. I still have it.

Anita, my father bought a book called *What Every Young Woman*

Should Know About Sex. He and my mother read the book together! Can you imagine? This is how my mother found out about sex and that it was "all right" to do it more than the few times when one wanted to conceive a child. My father tried to explain: "It is the best way we can *love.* Can we try to find our way to this goal together . . . without your being afraid of me?"

They tried, Anita. Both of them. Valiantly. But of course the damage had already been done. My mother was terrified. It was only accentuated by her vivid understanding that her older sister had died in childbirth. Mother could read the book, understand the words and diagrams, allow my father's attempts at helping her to learn to love sexually . . . but those lessons were hard to learn! Frightening! Horrifying!

But this is true: Mother determined she would not become bitter like my grandmother. My father was kind, gentle, tender with her, honestly praying with her about her fears. The first month that my mother's period was late, my father spent an entire day praying and fasting for a menstrual flow to ease her panic about having a baby until it was "asked of God." God answered prayer, *that month!* The next month she knew she was pregnant. She wasn't ready for a baby. "Ask and ye shall receive" had been a trusted Scripture verse. She had not asked, but she was receiving in spite of every human instinct screaming against it. For the first time in her book-loving, romantic, idealistic life, she did not understand God or His ways.

In spite of her determination to accept these new, unexpected events, depression haunted her. In her inner darkness, she was certain that when the baby was born, she would die as her sister before her had. She admitted that she wished for it. We who know her best believe she would have died following the birth . . . except for prayer! Only last week I received a letter from a lady who had been a child in my father's church. She wrote, "I remember that my parents were going to the church to pray for Sister Wood at 2:00. My aunt was to stay with me. We understood that the beautiful, gentle woman we had learned to love might die. I remember that, instead of playing, we walked about the house and yard together, praying with the adults in the church that Sister Wood would live. When my parents came home, their faces were glowing, assuring us that a miracle had occurred." Mary Gibbs concluded her letter, "Do you know anything about this experience?"

Did I know! My mother had determined that she would share everything with me, her only daughter, her youngest child. I've heard the story a dozen times. Mother said she was sinking so deep in pain that she felt she *was* pain. "I thought there could be no release. And then there was the feel of a large Hand touching me from head to toe and, in the touch, there was heat, which gave a warm healing to all my pain. I opened my eyes, smiled, and asked for my baby." It may have been a physical healing. It could have been an emotional healing. Neither my mother nor I ever knew or cared. *The miracle happened!*

There was not another baby for five years. Joe was the one child "asked of God." She was ready for a second child, eagerly wanting, waiting for his birth. God and sex finally made sense to my mother in the joy of this birth.

Fourteen months later, she gave birth to a third boy. God and sex again confused her, but this time she accepted the tiny redheaded infant with a heart full of love for his uniqueness. She told me, however, it made her sad that Joe, still a baby, had to be removed from her lap and her close attention. God and His ways were not as simple as she had once believed!

My mother passionately loved her three boys, rejoiced in them, and put them in a little red wagon every morning, when weather permitted, to take them on a trip where they would sit together and she would tell Bible stories, illustrating with stones, stick figures, and a mirror for seas, lakes, and rivers. She sang with them, laughed with them, played with them, challenged them to make scrapbooks where, in illustrating Scripture verses with magazine pictures, they happily memorized entire chapters that each of them can quote verbatim to this day! And Mother finally could thank God fervently for His wisdom in giving her these three distinct personalities, praying to be the best mother possible to them.

And what about their marriage during those years? My father adored my mother and *she knew it*! In the difficult learnings and adjustments from single independence to marital unity, she tried, with Daddy, to learn to *love* in sexual fulfillment.

When Daddy was fifty-three and Mother was forty-four, they discovered she was pregnant with me! They were both flabbergasted, confused, and embarrassed by all the jokes of "Abraham and Sarah" that became a medley that even I remember hearing. But in time they discovered, in Mother's words, "You were God's best gift to us in this time of our lives." I can still feel the touch of her hand on my hair and see her smile. "You keep us young!"

It was true. I was a dramatic dynamo, an exuberant spirit of laughing life. In spite of the real generation gap, both my parents were determined to "learn my generation," understand it as best they could, and rejoice in it. There were some hard times, but the truth is, we were the Three Musketeers. All my life, my elderly parents were my best friends!

Back to facing sex at forty and into the future, I am giving this long example because I know this sex story going into the eighties best. Of course, I am only sixty, too young to testify about sex in my eighties personally! But remember, my mother told me everything.

The last seven years of her life, she required skilled nursing care. My brother Joe and I went to visit during that crisis time. She had been moved from the hospital to a semiprivate room. My brother looked it over and said to our father, "The church you have served will meet Mother's expenses. I will pay for the other half of the room so you two can always be together." Lyman was a minister; Elton was a missionary in the Cape Verde Islands; I was a college professor. Joe felt he was best able to handle such a financial load. And in his great loving heart, he did.

They still had their home. Daddy was vibrant, strong, active. He went daily, when weather permitted, to work in his beloved garden in the two acres Joe had purchased behind the home my parents had bought for their retirement. My father had two activities he loved: preaching and gardening. He still had the best of both worlds.

My father was "at home" with my mother in their own room with their own furnishings. As others cared for her in unique ways, my father assisted. They ate their meals together; they had family devotions together. They were happy! Living closest to them, I went every holiday to decorate their room, and on Thanksgiving and Christmas we put Mother in a wheelchair and took her home to a meal I prepared for all of us.

The major point I am trying to make in response to your letter comes here. My parents did not live together for their more than fifty years of marriage in perfect, uninterrupted sexual bliss! It began in terror . . . but they worked at it. Together. It was a deliberate choice.

In fact, they learned to love so vitally, so beautifully, that my mother shocked me one afternoon when we were alone together in the nursing home. Are you ready for this? I wasn't.

In her eighties, my mother studied me at length, then proclaimed, "I believe now that sex in marriage is God's best gift, second only to the gift of Jesus himself!" I could only gasp. She smiled. "I've thought about it a lot. That evaluation is remarkable, considering the fact that I entered into the sexual side of love so ignorantly, so fearfully. There were so many times I hated it so!" She took a deep breath. "It's been a long road Daddy and I have walked together from that unhappy beginning. From our physical union have come our lives' greatest achievements: our children." She touched my hand. "But you four were part of our lives for such a brief time . . . we had to release you to yourselves . . . then we had to go back to living life . . . just the two of us . . . and we discovered that in our most understanding and ununderstanding times . . . in our most joyful and in our deeply sad times . . . our physical union could best accentuate the constancy of our love, *getting our attention*, as it were, onto our unconditional love . . . spotlighting our human love which is, is it not, God's best gift to us, second only to the gift of Jesus himself?"

She laughed, tilting her head, her eyes dancing: "Do you know Daddy and I make love at least once a week, even now?"

I could only gulp my shock. *"Mother!* What do you mean? You have a private room . . . but nurses are free to enter anytime!"

I remember her delighted face. "I know, but does it matter? No one has ever caught us, and if they did . . . well, they'd understand. It's *important* for us to love like this!"

I know this is an unusual way to respond to your letter, but it seems to me it may actually answer your most fundamental questions best.

I laughed in empathy at every syllable of your honest sharing. I, too, remember little kids running in with exciting news and perhaps a *frog*! Hard to be like movie stars with little kids in the house!

Oh, Anita, of course there are times when there is a loss of sexual desire, especially when one is "doing it all," juggling a rising career with the demands of a partner and growing children. Bob and I don't have to do *that* juggling act now, but we still have heavy responsibilities that sometimes leave us too weary to do more than sleep in our beds!

But I've counseled long enough to know that consistent fatigue or even pain during intercourse are symptoms that may be physiological and a doctor should be consulted. I read somewhere that researchers at the Rutgers Medical School found that women in their forties and beyond who are sexually active suffer less vaginal deterioration than those who enjoy sex infrequently. The recommendation was intercourse at least three times a month . . . *to tone up the vagina!*

I laughed when I read that line! The whole image of muscle tone, so important to us women whose muscles are beginning to sag *everywhere*, seemed so funny to me!

And then I remembered that in my childhood, there were two single professional women in our church . . . only two . . . and I gasped at their daring autonomy in a coupled world. I remember, however, the times one of them would come to our parsonage to counsel with Mother in regard to female problems. I remember Mother's thoughtful response after the woman had left: "Somehow it does seem God created woman and man for the ideal dream of marriage. Even in the physical." And I, with my paper dolls in my hands, would observe her mind trying to work out her theology. I was too small to know what problem was causing her reflection, but I vividly remember her response in those specific counseling sessions.

This documents the fact that the sexual part of marriage, Anita, is *good for your health* . . . according to the experts! My mother, in a pain-riddled body in a nursing home, at eighty, felt it important enough to be enjoyed "at least once a week" for their physical, mental, emotional . . . and, yes . . . spiritual well-being!

When we discussed it later in more depth, she said, "Daddy says it makes me a sweeter girl!" I laugh now as I laughed then. I've always remembered it, and I've always proven it true! Bob and I remember it, and he sometimes teases, "Now you're a sweeter girl," and I assure him he is "a much sweeter boy"! Why, Anita? Because

I have come to believe in the decades since my mother's startling evaluation . . . that she was right. Sex is God's best gift to a marriage, next to Jesus himself.

And when I find myself too tired, too distracted, too concerned with other things, I remember that Mother said sexual union "accentuates the constancy of our love, *giving our attention*, as it were, to our unconditional love. . . ."

As a young woman, my own mother taught me that one does not have to have a young, vibrantly healthy body to find sex exciting and fulfilling. In her eighties, needing skilled nursing care for her physical needs, she believed God was wise and good in giving her the gift of sex. And she determined to revel in it as long as was possible on this earth!

It seems to me in this letter, Anita, I have told you everything I know about sex at any age, spotlighting the forty-time when your body may begin to change. My father said, "It is the best way we can *love*. Can we try to find our way to this goal together?"

When women come to me confessing, "I love him, but I just have no interest in sex. He is starting to complain and I'm really worried," I share my father's question to my mother long ago. I advise these women, "Talk about it! Consider rescheduling your lives, determining to have quality time at least once a week for the two of you alone. Have 'mini-honeymoons,' where even an overnight stay at a hotel with a formal dinner can re-ignite the excitement of youthful passion, the dizzying, dazzling happiness, the bomb-blasting joy! 'Getting your attention, as it were, on your unconditional love!' "

Frequency is not the point here. I copied this quote from some female author in her seventies who said, "Having started my adult life feeling guilty about too much sex, I'll certainly not end my days feeling guilty about too little sex." Little doesn't mean lesser. More doesn't mean better.

It is only the love expressed in the union when the timing is right that counts.

In our marriage, Bob and I find that exhaustion and work stress often put sex on a back burner. We laugh, "I want to . . . passionately . . . I just don't have that much energy!"

I would tell you this: There were many "quickies" in our youth, but now our lovemaking is more ardent and embellished, less hurried and more savored, more of an event. According to sex researcher Morton Hunt, the average time spent on sexual foreplay is fifteen minutes, and the average duration of intercourse is ten minutes. I admire the expert, but his twenty-five minutes may be totally inadequate for the luxury of love long proven, deeply forged through life-years together. In our experience, the majesty lasts long after the passion has passed. Bob and I whisper, touch gently, sometimes sing a bit, then often fall asleep nestled together in the stardust of magic. In these years, our marital union is our joy in the morning and afternoon probably more than in the traditional nighttime, because our bodies tire more quickly than they did in our youth.

My mother and I, two generations before you, can tell you that standing on a foundation of comfort, confidence, and trust, there is a lot of room to experiment and pursue the new, the unexplored. In couples long married, there is no longer the excitement of conquest but the joy of self-celebration. In these years, we feel so secure that we can play like giddy children.

Helen Gurley Brown has placed herself—in her books and *Cosmopolitan* magazine, which she has longtime edited—as the guru of the single girl. Of course, now she has been a wife for nearly forty years. But she calls marriage "the bran muffin of sex." It saddens me that the woman who has described in detail the excitement of sex as a single girl describes her marital union with an image as bland as a bran muffin. Sorry! This is not my experience! I, the ice-cream devotee, cannot choose any worthy metaphor from a bakery shop. No! I must go for a deluxe *hot fudge sundae with all the trimmings.* Oh yes, let me answer Helen Gurley Brown's metaphor in a trumpet evaluation that sex in marriage is *the most exquisite dessert of all!* But I still believe my mother said it best a generation ago: *Sex is God's best gift to a married couple, next to Jesus himself.* If we choose to accept the gift with awed reverence, holy respect, and joyful gratitude, it will bring our own private, special splendor. Bob and I know!

Anita, thank you for inviting me to discuss this personal, private matter with you. I hope this unexpected storytelling may be my best answer to your letter. And here is the bottom line of what I would say: Sex in marriage—what a beautiful gift! Keep it Priority. Open yourself to the *magic of fireworks-splendor.* A woman from another generation promised it worth the effort in her old age in a nursing home. *This, too, is our own choice.*

—Moddy

Fighting Anger at Forty

ANITA HIGMAN

I told my friend the information about myself in confidence. Now it seems herds of people know about my secret. How can I continue to trust my friend?

I wasn't sure how to handle the situation, so I decided to be angry first.

It was a method of dealing with friendships that backfired like a beat-up jalopy, but for some reason it was still a way I sometimes cruised through life.

During the confrontation, my friend said softly, "I told the prayer chain about your situation because I care about you. And you never told me it was a secret."

Suddenly righteous indignation just didn't feel as simple and clean as it did before.

Life is complicated, I thought. *You would think at forty living would have gotten easier.*

· · · · · ·

MY DEAREST MODDY,

I admit it! I'm really angry right now! I'm sorry, but it's the flat-out truth!

It happens more often than I wish. I have kept thinking that by forty I'd surely have grown out of it. I thought forty birthday candles meant like, *whoof!* I'd be transformed into this calm-spirited angel who rarely churned up such passionately negative emotions.

Well, in my defense, I do have a few angelic flights, but other times my wings are singed from all the fiery darts I fling at the entire world, including my husband.

I guess you could say I do not step quietly into the night. Or morning, or any other time, come to think of it. People always *know* how I feel about everything. I have a big mouth, and I fear it is expanding proportionately to my advancing years.

But is this character aspect simply my God-given temperament, or is it something that must be dealt with in my spirit?

I do know there is a time for silence. *And* I know there is a time for speaking up. I just haven't figured out which one is appropriate in which situation.

Have you ever discovered a secret formula for how not to explode?

What about the times when you know you've been used, or treated unfairly, or had promises broken, or people are just plain thoughtless and rude to you? Those situations always seem to give such exquisite permission to go ahead and blast someone verbally. Feels great at the time, but I have to admit, I can't remember the blast ever feeling good later. It's usually only made everything more complicated and depressing.

I remember when some friends circled around me in confrontational anger about something I had done. Even when I began to cry, there was no mercy for me. I can still remember the piercing pain of that moment. It felt like a crushing steel anvil landing on my spirit. Instead of working things out, this incident was the beginning of the end of our wonderful friendships. I'd like to be able to recall that hurt when I get ready to verbally assault another person, even if that someone is indeed guilty.

But no matter who is at fault, I'd give anything if there were a little key in the brain that controlled anger. I mean, really, wouldn't it be great? When you sensed the emotions about to boil, you could just turn off the burner! It may sound goofy, but it would certainly make life easier and more pleasant. Why didn't God think of that?

I've often read Seneca's words, "If anger is not restrained, it is frequently more hurtful to us, than the injury that provokes it." I think that statement says so much, but I read it and still let anger fly!

Oh, Moddy, I'd love to be able to internalize his wisdom enough to live it for real. I could give out love always, and not only when it's convenient for me. My world would thank me. And so would my stomach!

I have countless stories to tell you about anger, but I'll share just one more. I remember years ago when I worked with someone who seemed almost impossible to deal with. If anything went wrong between us, I always felt I had to be the one to apologize. Mostly because the atmosphere became so unbearable. I didn't mind saying I was sorry some of the time, but I was not always at fault. In all honesty, it began to feel like we were trapped in some sort of sick game. She always played the hurter, and I always took on the role of the hurtee. She would sling the bitter hash, and I absorbed it. Anyway, I got *really* tired of it. If I appeared downhearted because of the stress between us, she thought I was manipulating her. If we talked it out, a new misunderstanding would suddenly pop up between us. If I did thoughtful things for her or gave her a little gift, she always thought I was up to something. I was weary of the abuse and being made to feel like something was wrong with me. Well, one day I blew up. Anger spewed forth like a grenade hitting a sewage tank. When it happened, she was shocked out of her gourd. But it didn't help. The ultimate release only proved to make the situation impossible. Even after words of forgiveness from both sides, I finally left the job. And though I didn't have to face the problem anymore, I always wished I could have come up with something more clever than anger to close our working relationship.

What do you think about anger? What about taking endless abuse? Is there a time to be angry? Can anger be presented with love? Is there such a thing?

You know me well enough to know that I try to see all of life's hues, but sometimes you know I *only see red*! *Sorry about that*! Oh, I do love you for letting me tell you these things I would never tell anybody else! I want to control anger, but it's so hard for me! Any help?

—Your loving but not
always saintly kid,
Anita

Don't Let It Dominate You

RUTH VAUGHN

I was there, observing the entire scene.

It had been a pleasant lunch, until a teasing remark ignited an unexpected rage. I saw the red flush of anger rise in my friend's face as her sister unexpectedly jumped to her feet screaming unfair accusations. She grabbed her coffee cup and threw it against the cabinet, followed by the saucer and a plate. As if smashing china wasn't enough, she shrieked her fury and rushed out of the house, slamming the door. My friend had not spoken during the tirade; nor did she speak now. She didn't even move. She just sat there until the flush of anger began to recede.

"It is not irresistible!"

I gaped my astonishment. *"What* did you say?"

She looked at me with a small smile of joy. "My sister and I grew up in an angry home. Shouting insults, throwing things, slamming doors was our way of life. When I went to college, I observed the price of my behavior. Not only did anger keep me unhappy, I had no friends. The first week my roommate moved out and no one else moved in. But I had no control. *Anger was just part of who I was.* That was that.

"One night in a church group where premarital sex was being discussed, the concept that in our youth sex is *irresistible* was challenged. Nothing is *irresistible.* Everything is a choice. Even in moments of great passion, one can choose to *resist.*

"With those words came the stunning insight: *The same thing is true of anger. Like sex, passionate feelings of anger do come at moments,* but what I do with it *is my choice. I can live by decision, rather than by emotion.* Since that time, I've used one word to hold me steady. I whisper that one word to myself over and over until I can calm down: *Resistible! Resistible! What I do with anger is my choice.*"

My eyes filled with tears of amazement and gratitude at my friend's strength, wisdom, and *chosen self-discipline.* I was privileged to bear witness.

• • • • • •

MY DEAR LOVING, NOT SAINTLY KID,

How I love your pure heart, your rigorous honesty. . . .

So . . . let's talk about anger! God created us with this passionate response. We find it in Jesus in the Temple! It seems that in some personalities He hand-stitched anger to have greater power than in others.

I remember a conversation I overheard of two women discussing my mother.

"She's a saint for sure. I'm around her a lot and I've never seen her angry, not even once. I wish I could be a Christian like that."

"Well, I am a Christian and I get angry all the time. It's all in personality types. Sister Wood was born sweet, calm, loving. I was born to speak my mind!"

I was in high school at the time, and remember stopping my activities in the room near the two women to ponder their words. I agreed with the first speaker. I lived with the woman, and I had never seen her angry. But my older brothers said they had glimpsed moments in their childhood. Was it personality or was it disciplined effort that made me, the child of her later years, find only the sweetness, the love, the compassion, regardless of life's injustices and pressures? It is now documented how personalities differ in response. But I still believe anger is a universal emotion. My father could erupt under heavy pressure or in the face of injustice in my growing-up years. I knew to walk softly on Saturday because that was the day of preparation! But Mother . . . was pure peace. She was sixty my sixteenth year, so she had many years of determining to *practice the presence of God*, her constant phrase. Anita, I believe Mother was no more saintly than any other earthling. In my study of her life in my sixty years of life, I believe it was her complete focus on God that made the difference.

I speak of my mother only from outside observation. The only thing I know to share with you about anger that is certain is my own experience.

Because I lived in a parsonage with parents fifty-three and forty-four years older than I, I rarely gave vent to anger in my home. I didn't observe it around me much, so as a small child I intuitively felt the need to discipline my own anger. I don't recall it ever being a problem until my teen years. . . . and then I could be *the most dramatically furious!* Not at home—such behavior was unacceptable there—but when something enraged me, I had a respite without anyone's knowledge. The parsonage was next door to the church. In the empty sanctuary, I could rush about the aisles dramatically screaming, shouting, weeping my fury at anything I considered unjust. Until my sixteenth year.

I have already told you of my creating a personal lexicon of word definitions that year. The one for love was: *I want what is best for you.* I began practicing that goal to the best of my ability, but I had little clue that those seven words had anything to do with my anger fits . . . until one afternoon.

I remember it vividly.

I've told you, too, that one of my brothers became seriously ill that year. He was able to come once from the Oklahoma hospital to our Texas parsonage. As I observed the brokenness of his successful life due to this illness, my fury spiraled. This particular afternoon, listening to my parents talking with my brother about his future, I rushed to the empty church, where I yelled to God my anger at the injustices He had allowed! It was all so unfair! The Almighty Sovereign could have prevented all this pain! So I eloquently, fervently, dramatically screamed at God, banging on His unseen chest at this injustice: the greatest I had known in my short life.

In a moment, taking time for breath, my recently written definition flooded my whole being, challenging me, taking my breath away: *I want what is best for you*. It stopped me silent in my tracks. It reeled in my brain like a phonograph record.

I had written those words so sincerely, so honestly, so piously . . . did I mean them? Well, of course I did . . . but what could that possibly have to do with my being justly angry in the face of gross injustice? I sat cross-legged in the middle aisle of the empty sanctuary and became very still.

I want what is best for you. Where was the relevance here?

Solemnly, carefully, I considered. Using all this time, all this energy in fury at the suffering in the life of my family . . . was this doing *what was best* for those I loved? Well, what else could I do?

I knew the answer. I could give the time I was spending venting my anger on practical things in my home . . . in this way giving relief to my parents . . . comforting them any way I could. And my brother? Well . . . he was strong enough to go to the Malt Shoppe for ice cream . . . and that would take his mind off his perplexing problems as he joined his small sister to chat about things that a sixteen-year-old would discuss with a much-older brother.

Perhaps it was then that I began to think about *time* initially . . . for I remember sitting silently in the middle aisle of the church . . . understanding that I could spend the next hour shouting my anger . . . or I could *feel* the anger but give it to my Creator, who understood all about the injustice . . . and my natural human response . . . and then let the anger pass through me, so I could use my *time and energies* in a more constructive way.

That would prove my faithfulness to my definition of love: *I want what is best for you.* That would put words into action.

I knew what was best for my family would be to give love, comfort, happiness to these three whom I loved and who needed these things, even from a sixteen-year-old.

My brother remembers the afternoon when I bounced into our home, hugging my parents, then laughingly inviting him for a chocolate shake. All these years later, we speak of the serendipity of that hour when we both ran away from the pain-filled present to talk of other things, even getting to know each other in new ways. He had gone to college when I was three, and I had never known him well, though I loved him deeply. Anita, we both believe today that in that hour—perhaps for the first time—we learned to respect, love, and know each other in new and meaningful ways.

And it taught me something important about anger. Since that time, I have known that when *I so choose* I can let my rage pass right through me. I know it can be done, for I have done it countless times.

I have seen it work for the trivial things, such as ruining a new white suit by spilling chocolate on it. Or when it rains on the day of a picnic. It holds true in my constant battle with my computer. When I was first exposed to this marvel, I could spend hours creating an entire document and with some slip of the finger, the whole thing would go into oblivion. I can still do it after all these years, to the amazement of my mechanical-genius husband.

God did not create me for computers! There is rarely a day that we don't fight in some way. But I have learned that when I lose hours of work in a finger slip, I look at the blank screen, accept its emptiness, and then with barely a heart flutter, I simply begin over again with word one . . . having come to believe (and prove) that the second, third, or fourth draft will be better than the original! Anger even in the trivial *can* flow right through you, allowing you to move on with the task at hand.

Humor helps a lot. I often say God created me because I am so inept at so many things that He, with all the *serious* problems of engineering sun, moon, stars, and the world with all of us imperfect creatures . . . would need a laugh sometimes. He can always find me good for a laugh! Because I choose to make *myself* good for a laugh.

Perhaps my best example was a time when my daughter-in-law was in intensive care in an Oklahoma City hospital while my brother lay in intensive care in a hospital on the other side of town. I was the only family member available on site for these precious two! I did my best.

One morning, about 2:00 A.M., I was with Penney when the Bethany hospital called to tell me my brother had a new heart problem. I was advised to come immediately. I explained to the nurses in the OKC hospital. They assured me they would care for Penney, and I jumped in the car to race across the city. *And then* . . . in the midst of that wonderful role of being the Good Samaritan—when you think God would have blessed me with a shining halo—a blinking light on the dash showed that the car was *out of gas*! I couldn't believe it!

I looked wildly about and spotted a service station across the street. The car got to the entrance and died. Some men came out in the subzero weather to push it to the tank, then they went back to the warmth of the station, while I, shivering, pumped my own gas. This is true: I looked up at God, laughing. "You have the strangest sense of humor . . . but perhaps you truly needed a good laugh . . . so here I am! Pumping gas as I try to give love to people in diverse parts of the city . . . and, with you, I do find this moment *hilarious*!"

I am laughing now, as I always do at the memory. This is an honest example of my learning to respond to unpleasant situations by letting the anger flow through me so quickly that I move on with life . . . and often . . . in laughter!

That is the little stuff. When my brother was ill, with his future in an upheaval, it was the big stuff. I have been given decades since that sixteenth year in dealing with big stuff. What I have learned is that anger *can* just pass right through until grief gathers tightly into itself and in the most intimate laceration of pain takes a permanent place. And there is nothing to be done about it until *time with God* brings redemption.

I don't mean I smile all the time, laughing at every empty gas tank! Not at all! There are times when anger is appropriate, as Jesus proved when He sent the moneychangers from the Temple. The best way I have found to deal with it is honesty. When a surge of angry energy rises in the face of betrayal, an unexpected response from others, or unwanted event, I simply accept the volcano heat and let it flow through—understand it, own it, but try to allow it to pass through me. If it still boils, I try to hold my poise until I can talk to God about it, before I speak to anyone else. When I do this, I can speak with more wisdom . . . and, most often, I don't speak at all.

Sometimes, of course, that is impossible. In marriage, for instance, misunderstandings can flare up in a flash. I think such emotion is good if you each honestly communicate those feelings to the other. I think Bob gave me the best advice in our engagement year: "If we can always talk honestly, there isn't anything we can't resolve. But we have to be totally honest." That has been the key to the magical wonder of our marriage. We talk honestly, even in moments of anger.

When he finds me totally stupid or unkind, or I find *him* totally stupid or unkind in words or actions that hurt, we have made it a commandment that we talk about it for as long as it takes until we understand that neither of us *intended* to wound the other. And then we have the joy of making up, big time! And, Anita, we always do battle privately. If something pains us in front of other people (including children), we go on normally in a social context. Then when we get to the privacy of our bedroom, we can close the door and "have at it"! Sometimes in powerful confrontation. But we are totally honest. We may shout, but eventually we are simply talking until we resolve the problem and can pray together. If that sounds silly, it really isn't. We determined we would never go to sleep angry. There are times when we wonder if we will sleep at all that night, but we have kept true to our determination we made in the beginning. We continue to talk/fight it through until we "kiss and make up," concluding in prayer. It's not easy, but I can tell you, *it works.*

I may not have *the* answer to the problem of anger. I can only share with you what I, with God's help, worked out growing up with the parents I had as role models. And I do believe the most vital reason that I handled my anger in the personal way that I did was because I was facing the most complex and most unfair injustice I had thus far encountered at the age of sixteen.

And because I wrote down my definition for love as *I want what is best for you* in that same significant year, it has served me all these years until, at age sixty, it is as natural to me as breathing. Bob still can fume at a long red light when we are in a hurry. I spend that unwanted still-time in prayer or in singing! When I am in the car alone, I always either silently pray or loudly sing. When I am in the passenger seat listening to Bob verbally abusing a red light, I silently pray for those I love, or irritate him even more by singing the "Hallelujah Chorus." Oh, Anita, I know! I know that sounds so piously *silly* that I have debated writing it here . . . except it is true! This is what I do.

Why? Because, beginning at an early age, I formed the habit-pattern—in the face of the starkest painful injustice (or the triviality of a long red light) anger never controls me for long, because *I chose* early to feel it, all of it, and then let it pass through me. It can be done.

This is *my* answer. My love, you must choose your own. Just know that in all of life, you are loved by

—Your own Moddy

Fighting Bitterness at Forty

ANITA HIGMAN

The pebbles glistened in the tiny stream like gemstones. I guess I'm still just enough of a kid to pick one up in the off chance it really is a jewel!

Right next to the sparkly ones was a dark and sticky-looking stone. What could that be? I reached down to investigate. It was hard to tell if it was covered with an oily fungus or something even more disgusting.

Quickly I threw the stone back and reached for one of the pretty ones.

Was there a lesson here? It seemed there is always a lesson in these sorts of things.

The gunky stones reminded me of the way bitterness can occasionally coat my life. It makes people passing by, and sometimes even friends, drop me like a rock. It simply makes people want to reach for something lovelier.

At forty, I wonder . . . am I choosing to tumble through life with a sparkle, or am I too often just sitting there being disgusting?

• • • • • •

DEAR, DEAR MODDY,

I'm supposed to be good with words, yet what can I say to you, really? Even though we are expressing ourselves with words, I have found myself helpless this year in trying to express what these writings mean to me. And what *you* mean to me. So I'll just be simple. Thank you for this ever-flowing encouragement and love. Thank you, with all my heart.

But . . . I'm afraid I have a question that is another difficult one. I hope I'm not wearying you with my rushing out with the big questions that have haunted me a lifetime. I just trust you enough to believe you really do care and want to know.

Well, Moddy, here's one. I don't like the word. I don't like the feeling. But it's part of our language as it is a part of me. I hate it. Honest! Even when I say it aloud, my mouth is forced into a rather harsh position. Here is the word, Moddy: *bitterness*.

I must confess in all honesty that in my heart, bitterness jumps in to take residence way too easily. It's like a fungus sliming its way in, going unnoticed, until it has taken control of its host. First it may look tolerable, but before I know it, it has eaten away at everything lovely. It has left nothing but rot. I hate it, but this is true.

I use this analogy often because in Houston there are some wildly colorful-looking fungi. And here in this semitropical environment we have learned that fungus is not a fun guy! Anyway, one of them suddenly appears out of nowhere like a mysterious yellow goo. Actually, it looks very similar to a large dollop of paint. But later it dries, turns spooky brown, and then its dust spreads from here to kingdom come. I assume those are spores flying to the wind, which I also assume will then find another willing party to torture with its rotting ugliness. So, I truly want to try to throw out this funguslike thing called bitterness before it takes residence, finding me a willing host.

I try, Moddy. Hard.

You know that there are many hurtful things that happened in my youth and in my past in general. I know these things can destroy me if I let them. I'm staying above it now, but I do wonder sometimes if bitterness won't finally consume me.

I've been pretty good about it so far, Moddy. I remember years ago when I was sexually harassed within the company I was working for. It was humiliating and degrading and maddening. There didn't seem to be anything I could do about it. No one seemed to care about my plight. I was alone in my problem. I could have gotten very bitter, but I really handled that one pretty well.

I think through my life history as I write to you and find it littered with incidents in which people have mistreated me in some way. I do want you to know that I've succeeded in not becoming bitter about some, and that makes me happy. But there are some people problems over which I've not been triumphant. Bitterness creeps in because it seems so right, so just! Do you know what I mean?

I'm wondering. How do you handle it, in general? How do you clean it up once it's there? And then how do you keep it from cropping up again? I know I'm always looking for a formula, Moddy. If you have one, I'm willing to try it.

I don't want to grow old with a bitter tongue attacking others—indeed, attacking myself with the bitter fungus living in my heart. Can you help me? I do want to have a peaceful heart so I can speak gentleness, kindness, and love.

Life is unfair, Moddy! You know that as well as I do. I know Jesus went on loving when people spat on Him, jerked out His beard, and crucified Him. But He was the Son of God. I'm very, very human . . . please help me in my humanness.

I wish I could get your presence through e-mail. Since I can't, I'll send this letter by snail mail and ask you to read its confession in love. . . .

—Anita

Choose What You Will Remember

RUTH VAUGHN

Today was one of those days! I went to a luncheon wearing a Mickey Mouse T-shirt and jeans while everyone else was dressed in formal suits! I had forgotten the agreed-upon dress code. *And then,* during the conversation, I brought up a date that had been an excruciatingly painful time to one of them. Realizing my slip, my face reddened in embarrassment. *Today I should have stayed in bed!*

But my friend's eyes danced as she quickly picked up the conversational threads by saying, "Yes, I remember that time. It was the beginning of spring. I know because I went for a walk in the park in the late afternoon and a plump red robin came down and sat beside me."

Surprised at her handling of the situation, I asked about it on the way home. She smiled.

"I can't choose the experiences that come into my life, *but I can choose what I will remember.* For that time, I choose to remember the robin. I discarded the bitter words long ago."

She looked at me a moment and said thoughtfully, "Do you know, I honestly can't remember what was said! I wanted to then . . . and many times since I have wanted to pity myself by going back to that time and reviewing the pain, but I have always refused. When that time comes to my mind, I force myself to think about that red robin and how beautiful he was! Funny, I guess, but I do smile when I think of that time now . . . and I really can't remember the cruel words that were said."

My friend has chosen to cherish the treasures of life, but when unpleasant memories come to mind, she *remembers to forget.* Thank you, my friend, for your wisdom. I learn from you.

• • • • • •

ANITA, MY LOVE . . .

Your letter came today by "snail mail." Your suggestion of e-mailing me to Houston is great, but until Bill Gates comes up with that phenomenon, rest in this truth: There is no space in love. We are together as much as if I were holding you in my arms in your big chair!

Yes, bitterness is an insidious fungus. I like your analogy very much. In my youth, I lived near Houston for a time, so I understand the aptness.

Bitterness! A universal enemy! To all of us *humans*. We don't like it, but in spite of good intentions, *there it is*. So, what to do?

Anita, I believe Paul gave us the answer in 1 Thessalonians 5:16–18: "Rejoice always, pray without ceasing, in everything give thanks; for this is the will of God in Christ Jesus for you" (NKJV).

Let's consider this one small sentence to see if it *is the answer to bitterness.*

Perhaps my favorite "famous" example of one conquering bitterness may be that of the great Russian author, Alexander Solzhenitsyn. His bestseller, *The Gulag Archipelago*, is the account of the inhumanities of imprisoned Russians under Stalin. His observations are autobiographical, taken from his own experience.

In the Russian Gulag, he *chose* in those terror/pain-filled years to open his soul, his perception, his inner ears until he heard a divine voice so clearly that he changed from communistic atheism to the holy awe and daily companioning, *even then, even there*, of the faithful, abiding presence of the loving Father God. The majority of prisoners succumbed to the horrors of imprisonment psychologically, spiritually, often physically. But when Solzhenitsyn found the love of divine presence *in him, with him*, he moved in serenity, in service to others, rejoicing, praying, giving thanks for everything.

When he was finally released from prison and allowed to move to America, he wrote in perspective his profound account of the stark injustices meted out to him in every life dimension those years. Here is the startling sentence, Anita. In his book, Alexander Solzhenitsyn wrote, "Thank you, prison camp!"

Breathtaking, isn't it?

Introducing Solzhenitsyn at Harvard, Bernard Levin said, "Let me say that he is *the* most important living human being and the most ennobling . . . and yet I must totally dissociate myself from his theological views." Solzhenitsyn went to the lectern then to present his joyful, triumphant faith that all of his life was God's will for him in Jesus Christ! No one could silence his powerful testimony of a life *free of bitterness*. No one could keep him from reviewing the most horrible sufferings inflicted by humans on other humans the world could ever know, concluding, "Thank you, prison camp."

William F. Buckley Jr. said in an interview, "The influence of Solzhenitsyn is so palpable that no one can make him or it go away. It would be like trying to go through Elizabethan England as if Shakespeare did not exist. He is that much a presence. Now having gone through what he has gone through, now having a more vital, valid effect on the world than any other personality in this century by turning around political philosophy in Western Europe, he speaks always in accents that God is King . . . that Jesus Christ is the Incarnation. And yet this terribly pains those who cannot deny the impact of Solzhenitsyn, and yet are horrified at the great lengths to which he takes his own religious testimony.

"These people try to take it out of his impact and yet it is non-fissionable. They seek to take the one Solzhenitsyn (the political, literary giant) away from the other (the Christian) and they find this impossible."

Wherever Solzhenitsyn goes, he continues his joyful gratitude for all of life, even the hardest parts, for God was *with him*. Jubilantly he says simply, "Thank you, prison camp!" Anita, it was deliberate *choice* that made the difference!

As it was with Paul. Read the account when he was in jail with his back bleeding and his hands and feet in stocks, singing praises at midnight. He was not role-playing Pollyanna, Anita. He knew his body was hurting; the food was terrible; most of his roommates were disagreeable. Those were the facts; he could not *change* the facts. What he *could choose to change* was his response.

"Rejoice always," he wrote later, "pray without ceasing, in everything give thanks; for this is the will of God in Christ Jesus for you."

Anita, perhaps my favorite personal example comes from the life of my mother. I mentioned earlier that my childhood ended at the age of fifteen when my mother collapsed at our dinner table. She was unconscious for several hours. When she awakened, we understood she had been stricken with acute arthritis and could not move. Bedfast, her every need had to be handled as if she were an infant. Physically, that was true. Spiritually, I observed with teen-age clarity her *giant status*!

The small-town doctor believed that the collapse had occurred because of poisoned gums, so the dentist took out *all of my mother's teeth* and then pronounced the gums and teeth had been in perfect condition! By summer, my father took her to a health clinic. He had to go back home to pastor his church. I was completely responsible for her care when she was not in the clinic with doctors, nurses, and hot baths.

Anita, picture my mother that summer. The Wizard Wells baths and other treatments caused her body to swell to twice her size. She was *huge*! Every joint seemed frozen. She couldn't move. She had no teeth, so she couldn't eat without "gumming it." We stayed in a small apartment with no air conditioning. We had a hot plate, and an icebox to which ice had to be delivered in squares twice a week, melting into a pan underneath, which I always allowed to overflow!

At age fifteen, I cooked her special diet, grinding it up so she could eat it. It was dreadful, as you can imagine, with me as chef on a hot plate. I burned everything. And the food: lots of liver and spinach! Ground up, it looked and smelled gross! I spoon-fed her. I had to assist her every movement. For her to stand, I would pull her swollen, stiff body onto her mammoth feet, then she would place her hands on my shoulders and we would shuffle slowly—oh, so slowly—to the bathroom and back to the bed. At least once a day, I was instructed to place her facedown on the bed. I was a tiny, petite teenager, and one afternoon when I was striving to put her onto the bed facedown, I missed, and my mother fell heavily from the bed to the stark cement floor . . . on her face.

Oh, Anita, I knew I had killed her! I raced to the nearby hospital screaming, as doctors rushed to the apartment. "I'm so sorry, Mother! Please, don't die! Please, forgive me! Oh, I am so sorry!" As the men stood her upright, instead of raging at me as any normal human being would have done, my mother astonished all present by looking at us and bursting into laughter. "Oh my! I guess I'm like Goliath after David's slingshot blow." Even with no teeth, she dramatically exclaimed, "And great was the fall thereof!"

In all that pain, in all that humiliation, in all that swollen stiffness, *my mother laughed!* How could she do that? I can tell you. She had based her life philosophy on Paul's words: "Rejoice always, pray without ceasing, in everything give thanks; for this is the will of God in Christ Jesus for you."

One hot summer night I sat beside my mother's bed quietly pondering her life and her astonishing responses to it. I asked,

"Mother, why do you act like you do? Why don't you seem to mind the injustice of this sudden, unexpected break in your health that is completely destroying your active, loving, giving life as a minister's wife?"

She gave me that sweet smile of hers. "Oh, honey, of course I mind!" There was a long silence before she spoke the words engraved on my heart forever: "I mind for myself very much! But when I keep focused on the love of my faithful husband, the glowing achievements of my three sons, and the way my little girl is growing toward maturity, I am *cushioned by gratitude.*" Tears spilled down my cheeks in that moment as they do at this moment in my Oklahoma City home writing to you at my computer.

My mother—that year and in that place—*consciously chose* to focus on the good stuff, although the bad stuff had stripped her of her health, her teeth, her freedom of movement, and an active, productive life as a minister's wife. It was all gone! I was there, Anita, observing twenty-four hours a day, seven days a week. She could have, should have been *bitter*! It was so unfair: not only the stiff, swollen body but the misdiagnosis that cost her a healthy set of teeth! I never once heard her complain. I kept waiting for it, but there was not a syllable of bitterness. Because there was no emotion of bitterness. She knew bitterness would destroy her. She fought it until it slithered away. Bitterness or betterness? *It was her choice!*

The first time someone asked me to describe my mother's response to that year of severe illness, I surprised us both by saying, "Well, she laughed a lot!"

I've always remembered my spontaneous response. It was true. I was the person closest to her pounding pain, her humiliating circumstances in which a fifteen-year-old had to care for her like an infant, in the unforgiving heat, bringing water from a pump like in the eighteenth century! I remember it all, but only as background.

My mother centerstaged my memory with "She laughed a lot!"

Can you imagine how unpleasant she could have made that year, especially that summer at Wizard Wells, alone with a small, inept, untrained child as her nursemaid? She could have been filled with justified self-pity. She could have injected me with bitterness for a lifetime. She could have made everyone around her unhappy. Instead, she had me gather up the children in the small village every afternoon. I would sit her up in a great chair, filled with pillows. There she would tell stories, sing with the group around her on the stone floor, and even do finger plays with swollen fingers that could barely move. She was indomitable.

From her earliest youth, she *chose* to know that faith was greater than fate; character was superior to circumstances. God was with her. She was safe there. Life's circumstances were harsh but she could smile in them for she *chose* to be cushioned by gratitude for all the wonderful things that were still true!

I think my best answer to your letter may be in sharing these examples of people just like you and me who have faced things neither of us know . . . but they were strong, serene, joyful, even then, even there. Why? There is only one answer, Anita. They *chose* to focus on God's will in Jesus Christ who challenged them to *choose* to give thanks in everything!

Solomon wrote, "A relaxed attitude lengthens a man's life; bitterness rots it away." Choice: life or death . . . sweetness or bitterness. I can tell you that Alexander Solzhenitsyn, the apostle Paul, and my mother determined to *choose wisely*.

The challenge is ours, Anita . . . every moment, every day, every year. Let's covenant together to *choose wisely* in our own lives. It's such a hard lesson to learn, but let's determine to learn it!

—Moddy

Fighting Worry at Forty

ANITA HIGMAN

It all started with an innocent bit of concern. Most horrific worries can start out that way.

Anyway, I took time out from my busy day to play with the concern in my head. I let the concern bug take a couple of steps toward me, though I deliberately tried not to notice.

Later that day I fed my concern by thinking of all the "what if" scenarios that could turn my concern into a real worry.

Guess what? Suddenly this creature became a three-headed monster. I didn't even need to ask its name. It was Worry.

The friends who said, "Pray about the problem," or "You're blowing this situation out of proportion," were ignored. I was now in a quest for some clear-thinking person like myself who could see the bigger picture and know that I truly had ample reason to sweat.

Funny, even though I'd now received a generous helping of "age" didn't mean I had a goodly portion of common sense to go with it.

I decided it was time for a writing chat with Moddy. She has enough horse sense for both of us!

· · · · · ·

DEAR MODDY,

It's me again!

I had determined to write a cheerful note asking about your life, about the backyard Bob is creating with ponds and a "singing stream" flowing beneath a "kissing bridge," as you jubilantly wrote to me recently. I was going to respond in kind, but I'm sure you're dancing to the singing stream and kissing your handsome husband on the little bridge . . . so I'll just go ahead and write what I need to write! Thanks for letting me know that's OK!

Well, here goes! Ready?

Tell me, dear Moddy, do you ever find yourself wringing your hands in worry? I do, and too often. I don't see Peter fussing over every little thing. Just me mostly. I have enough material to strain on for several lifetimes. Need any extra?

And I'm beginning to think that worrying begets worry. If I allow myself a little stew, I end up getting the whole pot!

I've succumbed to worrying about even the dinky things in life. As they say, molehills become mountains. And for me, molehills seem to surround me just waiting to get bigger. And I am always there ready to comply.

When I was in junior high and high school, I remember tearing myself up over my grades. I had one teacher tell me I'd end up with ulcers. I didn't, but I really did sweat those grades. I turned out to be valedictorian in both junior high and high school. But I paid the price, and not just in hard work. That would have been acceptable. But I was doubly worn out, because worry accompanied the work. And so it has continued throughout my life—my being a constant companion to that thing called worry.

"Worry is the unwelcome guest who keeps returning at our request." Doesn't that sound nice? I can tell you it's almost impossible to put that pearl of head knowledge into my heart and daily activities.

I want to internalize this so much because over the years this thing has been like living with emotional constipation. I just feel dragged down all the time, as though I need a good cleansing of the spirit.

Even if I try to turn off the worry-churning, it's only like shooing flies. The nasty critters just keep coming back. First they swarm around, and then they get bold again and land their filthy little feet right on my pretty pink frosted cake. In other words, worry is a hard varmint to get rid of. And as much as I hate to confess it to you, it's often downright impossible!

I've discovered I can't have much fun when I'm worrying. Oh, I can pretend, but it's only an act, a mask covering a heart heavy with anxious clutter. In fact, it makes me physically ill at times. I have to go to bed!

I think God should have created each of us with a box and a timer to control worry. Think about it! When worry dashes in, we could take it out of its box at the appointed time, worry a bit, then put it back. Kind of like exercise. Schedule it, do it, then forget about it.

But if God put that timer on some people, he left it out of me. Completely. Worry is like a disease with me. It affects everything and follows me everywhere. It doesn't care if I am watching the sun go down in splendor, or giving a speech, or trying to laugh around the table with my kids. It's there, always intruding upon my life.

Then when you add being forty to the mix . . . Wow! It's just a bit more complicated than the poet makes it. Adding to my usual worries, now that I'm forty, I have to worry about topics like aging and illness and the kids' college education and retirement monies! I'm afraid it's all making me bug-eyed with fretting misery.

Funny, too, I'd have thought that the older I got, the more tired I'd get of putting up with worry's strenuous obligations. I guess I was hoping one day I'd just go to bed and say, "I can't take this anymore. Living is too valuable to waste it sweating everything under the sun. I'll just give it to the Lord once and for all. And I'll never take any of it back."

Then I'd wake up the next morning and know it was a genuine promise. Not only for my benefit, but for my family and friends and the rest of the people on this earth who will have some dealing with me between now and eternity. Not to mention the fact that I know it would please God for me to be free of worry.

Doesn't that goal sound great? How can I make that a daily life reality and not just a pipe dream? I know that's a tall order, Moddy dear, but do give me words of wisdom from sixty years of living a life that I know has had to be littered with worries! Like me, when I was eighteen and so silly. I seem to recall your once saying you watched me and prayed for me with a wistful heart. Why was your heart wistful? Because, of course, you found my immaturity something significant to worry about! You had to wonder if I'd ever grow up. Well, I'm not grown up yet, but I'm working at it. And you're helping me so much by taking all that time and energy to respond to my every letter, whether trivial or significant. Well, this is so significant, I've waited till now to finally ask you about it. Moddy, is there an "answer" to worry?

Speak. Your Anita will listen. Carefully. Why? Because I need you to speak. I trust you to love me enough to help your forty-year-old kid

who's tired of being a good sport
at playing the old worrywart!

We Are What We Think

RUTH VAUGHN

She was unhappy. There were taut lines about her eyes. Although she smiled and laughed in her chatter, I knew she was unhappy.

When the door finally closed behind the last guest, she sank into the big armchair and said, "I'm so worried! About everything! I worry about the world situation. I worry about Don losing his job. I worry about . . ."

"Is Don's job in jeopardy?"

"Oh no! Everything is all right . . . *now*. In fact, he got a raise last week. But *what if* . . . he loses his job? What would we do? We wouldn't have a roof over our heads!" She sighed. "Oh, Ruth, I really do trust God! It's just that I'm so worried!"

Her brows knit in fear and she seemed unaware of the incongruity of her last remark.

I remembered John Wesley once said, "I would no more fret and worry than I would curse and swear." Early in my life, my mother had begun to teach me about John Wesley's conviction of the *disobedience of worry* in the life of God's children. If God is our Father, we are *secure in all circumstances*. Is worry SIN?

The concept shocked me long ago. Now I took my Bible and showed my friend a little poem I had scrawled on its flyleaf. "I wrote this in my youth; *it is my faith*."

She read it aloud:

"My world is an uncertain thing,
Changing from day to day;
Politics and economy

Forever shift and sway.
But He who holds the universe
Is taking care of me.
And so I rest in peace and quiet . . .
This is security!"

We talked all afternoon. Worry is a constant warrior *unless we choose* its defeat!

• • • • • •

MY PRECIOUS, TIRED WORRYWART!

I understand every syllable of your letter in your concern over your worry bouts. As far as I can tell, it *is* chiefly a gender problem. Most men do not choose to spend their time in nail-biting worry. Only we women. And men cannot understand why we punish ourselves like this.

Recently I found this entry in an old journal: "I am thinking of the child's story 'Chicken Little,' who shrieks false fear: 'The sky is falling! The sky is falling!' I'm afraid that is *me* today! I'm so filled with the 'what ifs' of my worst nightmares that my heart is pounding. . . . I know I can *choose* trust over worry, but it's so *hard!"*

This is the next entry: "I've just been studying these words: 'Don't worry about anything; instead, pray about everything; tell God your needs and don't forget to thank him for his answers' (Philippians 4:6–7, TLB). 'Let [God] have all your worries and cares, for he is always thinking about you and watching everything that concerns you' (1 Peter 5:7, TLB).

"Oh, God, will you help me with this worry thing? *'Don't worry about anything!'* That's a command, isn't it? I want to obey, but it is so difficult! Help me, please!"

Webster's defines worry as "undue mental disturbance caused

by anxiety, vexation, fears with little or no foundation." In my personal lexicon, I define worry as "the anxious state of having a fit of 'what ifs'!" Instead of banishing them, I can let the fits fly . . . too long . . . too long. . . .

Like you, I became a highly skilled worrier! It must have been at this time that I wrote the above journal entries. Neither this page nor the entire journal is dated, one of my problems in earlier years. My brother Elton only recently has gotten me to date letters!

But, Anita, when I began to study these verses, memorized in childhood, and understood that they clearly phrased a command as explicit as the traditional Ten in Exodus, I prayed for divine assistance in order to obey this most difficult command: "Don't worry about anything!" Wow!

Has there ever been a time in my life when there were not a million "what ifs" to worry about? No! I assure you from my journal records that age only brings different "what ifs." They are like vultures coming. No matter one's age.

Yet there is the command, "Don't worry about *anything*!"

How to obey?

The answer that works for me is in Proverbs 23:7 (KJV): "For as [a man] thinketh in his heart, so is he. . . ." When I made a personal paraphrase, the answer to worry clicked in!

"As Ruth thinks in her heart, so is Ruth!"

The first time I wrote that out, I stared and stared and stared. "Worry *is a choice*!" I wrote, "There are so many horrors in my close observation of others, so many terrors threatening me, my family, my loved ones at any moment that I could get lost in the insecurity of the 'what ifs,' unless I choose to focus on this divine analysis. I don't believe this is a psychological concept arrived at by any man. God simply states we are *not* what we think we are. Instead, indeed, *we are what we think*!"

Note the verb "think," which is a function of the mind. Emotion is a part of it, too, because "as [a man] thinketh *in his heart*. . . ." Here we are commanded to use our minds and more. He means the central core of our very selves, our mind-hearts. That is where we feel, where we will, where *we choose how we think*!

Every moment, every day, even in the midnight watches, it is a choice.

I know. I know because I understand the demands of this personal decision. When I get caught in the tornado of the "what ifs," I *can choose* to focus my entire mind on the words of an old hymn learned as a child—now my literal lifeline: "O, to be like Thee! blessed Redeemer. . ." and concluding: "Stamp Thine own image deep on my heart."

Anita, when worry over the many future "what ifs," worry that my words or actions could be misinterpreted by others, worry over *anything* grips me like a mouse in a cat's paw and I am helpless in its power, I *can choose to hold steady*—the terrified little mouse—and sing those words.

Actually, I don't like to sing "O, to be like Thee! . . . Stamp Thine own image deep on my heart." In all honesty, Anita, I would rather let my mind continue to explore all the anxious areas of my life over which I have no control. I would *prefer* to do that. Sometimes I still give in to the luxury of a worry panic. But more and more I find that as I force myself to whisper softly—or loudly sing—my prayer, I slip from the cat's paw of worry, and as God's child I can face life as it is. The key is

"As Ruth thinks in her heart, so is Ruth!"

When I make my thoughts even narrowly focus on the small chorus-prayer, *it changes me*! Only last night, I lay back in the recliner in the den, extremely weary, physically unwell, and the tornado of "what ifs" from a dozen different directions grabbed me in its vortex until I was almost frantic. Anita, I knew the answer. I can give up the luxury of being the victim . . . alone . . . or in worry parties if others will worry with me. The choice is mine.

So, with a deep breath of regret, I gave total focus to the words of this prayer-chorus and within minutes the tornado had blown away. I knew some of those "what if" horrors might be mine within the week, but, if so, they would only give me better opportunity to live out this prayer, even to those who might be unlovely in response. I could wring my hands in worry, I could cringe in fear with little or no foundation (or even with a quite-possible foundation)—or I could choose to obey the divine command: "Do not worry about anything." And while this is impossible within the human psyche (especially the female psyche) without divine power, we have the formula for not worrying: "As we think in our heart, so are we!"

> "As Ruth thinks in her heart, so is Ruth!"
> "As Anita thinks in her heart, so is Anita!"

If those thoughts are thrust into narrow focus on the words of the old prayer-chorus, we can be "more than conquerors" over all the "what ifs" of our lives, no matter our age, no matter our circumstances, through Him who loves us!

My beloved child, this is the only answer I know to worry.

—Moddy

Facing Fear at Forty

ANITA HIGMAN

If worry is like an insect, then fear is the animal that eats worry for lunch.
Yep. That's seems to cover it.

Fear doesn't sashay. It lunges. And I have been the object of that lunging.

I get a bit of comfort from the fact that I am not alone. Everyone else has been lunged at too. It is a fact of this earthly sojourn.

Some time ago I was doing a little snorkeling in the Caribbean when the ocean waves suddenly seemed to overtake me. I grabbed a rock in terror and clung for dear life. I don't know what people mean when they say your whole life flashes before you when you think you're dying. I was too busy trying to stay alive to think through the past!

Obviously, I survived the ordeal, but I sometimes ponder fear. I can't help but wonder how it will interact with growing old.

Does it diminish with age? Or will it continue to get fat on thin air?

· · · · · ·

OH, MODDY!

I'm so scared just now!

Fear. Pure fear throbs every corpuscle. I thought worry was a big deal, but suddenly FEAR has slapped me in the face. Hard.

It's three in the morning. I could not sleep. I kept touching Pete to be sure he was all right. Finally I went to the kitchen table, fixed some tea, and knew I had to write to you. Oh, please understand me, please help me!

In our last letters, we did some pretty good stuff on worry, didn't we? I've been feeling satisfied, maybe even smug about thinking I could begin to handle worry, but I've decided that fear is "worry on steroids." That's a good definition, don't you think?

Fear has moved in so intensely and quickly, it's like looking through binoculars and watching rabid dogs chase after something . . . then realizing too late, they're coming after me! Well, their sharp teeth are in my heart right now. *I am so afraid!*

Moddy, it happened yesterday. I responded in every way I knew to help. When I finally got home and it was time to put the kids and Peter to bed, fear grabbed me by the throat! While my husband is sleeping, I'm coming to you. Tonight I am so afraid.

Yesterday one of my friends kissed her husband good-bye as he drove off to a normal day of work. A speeding car ran a red light and my friend's husband was killed instantly. In response to one knock on her door by a policeman, everything, everything changed about her life forever! I grieve for her! But I totally panic for *me!*

Moddy, this could happen to Peter today. Just the thought of it makes me want to throw up. I really may be sick. I'm not just afraid, I'm terrified!

How dare God? Oh, Moddy, is that awful to say? Will He strike me dead here in my kitchen for such a thought? But it's so unfair. Isn't it? Will I live in this kind of fear of God for the rest of my life?

This degree of fear is new to me. Maybe I've lived a charmed life or something, but so has my friend! We're the same age—grew up, college, marriage, kids. Normal! Everything in her life has been as normal as my own. Now, in a millisecond, nothing is or will be normal again. I've seen it on TV, of course, but this is my dear friend, Moddy, and it could be me tomorrow! I am crying as I write you. I am so scared!

Now I look at what I've written and it sounds really dumb. Of course I've known fear before. I've had horrifying childhood accidents, including the time my brother unintentionally hit me in the head with a baseball bat. Even as an adult, I've been afraid of being killed. Did you know I was in an airplane that caught fire over the ocean? Another time I was mistaken for a deer in the woods by a hunter! I could have died!

Of course, our kids always scare us too. When Hillary was very small she climbed up high on the swing-set ladder. Before I could get to her, she fell to the ground. I was terrified and grabbed her, screaming. She was more scared than hurt, but I kept hugging her tightly and crying so much, she soon became more frightened of my crying than of her pain. It wasn't easy to get over the sheer nightmare of that moment and what could have happened. It took me a while before I calmed down.

But this week I see up close that the real thing can happen. Forever loss can occur in the most normal life. Including my own. With no notice!

She kissed him like she had on a thousand mornings. She knew exactly what her future would be. Without a moment's warning, everything changed! I think of Peter and I tremble as the tears flow. Isn't fear legitimate here? I mean, this could happen to me. Oh, Moddy, I'm filled with such fear I don't know if I can leave this kitchen table tonight. Loss came to a woman I know. It could happen to me, and I am *so* scared!

When I first began to write these serious forty-letters, I told you the biggie for me was fear of the unknown. This is my first confrontation up close of how cruel that unknown can be!

I mean, really, my big fears have been of growing old! That's an unknown, too, and I don't like it. I don't want to get old, wrinkled, and—if I live long enough—even feeble and crippled. I don't want that! Moddy, in every area of my life tonight, what I'm feeling is not worry. It is pure, honest *fear*! I've just been slapped in the face with the cold, hard fact that I can't control my life. I can't hold the present—with my loved ones healthy and Peter and me forever young. I could lose one or all of them tomorrow. I know this, and I sob at the kitchen table in fear of the unknown.

I've calmed down enough to dry my face, fix another cup of tea, and see if I can think more coherently. This is not only fear of grief, it's fear of *change*. That's the bottom line, isn't it? Not only fear of sudden loss in my family, but part of my terror is this whole business of mid-life, isn't it? Being forty, moving into the "last of life" is *change*, Moddy, and I don't like it! No matter how optimistic Browning is in his lines, I'd rather keep living in the "first half of life."

I got up to walk around the kitchen—trying to think clearly what I'm really feeling, trying to phrase something that makes sense enough to ask you to help me in this moment of such fear.

I've finally sat down, finished my tea, and I'll try to be more lucid. I think I've come up with two simple questions I want to ask: "Can I be sure God loves *me*?" and "Is He really watching out for me and my family?" From years of attending church, my head knows the right answers to these questions, but you know it's easier to believe when all is going well in life. But they aren't going well in my friend's life right now—and it could happen to me!

Is there any hope of living confidently again? Does that sound too dramatic? Everything has changed for my friend, and in this moment fear has changed everything for me. I'm shaking. Head knowledge won't do it! How do I get all that good stuff I've learned about God through the years to root deeply into the core of my heart and give me confidence in a life where the unknown lies waiting? Without warning. Without preparation. Life isn't fair, Moddy, and I'm afraid!

I sit here and think of you. You've had some terrifying "unexpecteds" happen to you personally. When I think of your life, I can't imagine how you have coped. When I heard news bulletins of the losses in your life, everyone told me you smiled on. But, Moddy, you've got to know about fear. Everybody knows fear. How did you deal with the verse "God is love"? Do you think my friend believes God is love tonight? Does He love her and her children in a special way, even though she sleeps alone?

"Perfect love casts out fear." I'm afraid I don't really know what that means. How does love "cast out fear" in my life tonight? In my friend's life? I know a lot of Scripture, Moddy. It's easy to memorize pretty words, but what do they mean?

I'm calmer now. I think I'll go to bed soon. I'll close by asking something that may sound stupid, but I'd like your answer. Do you know about fear? When did you first know *real* fear? What have been your answers to it?

Oh, Moddy, please love your own Anita who's trembling in the night. . . .

Perfect Love Does Cast It Out

RUTH VAUGHN

I opened the letter, handwritten on navy blue stationery. It began:

DEAR MRS. VAUGHN,

Although I've never seen you, I want to thank you for your gift to me. Let me explain: I'm fourteen, and I have cerebral palsy with the prognosis that I will eventually have to be in a wheelchair. I've been so terrified, Mrs. Vaughn. I've wondered if life were worth living! Today one of my friends sent me a copy of your magazine article entitled "Thank You for Saying No!" As I studied its concept over and over, I finally began to sob, accepting these words as the *key to my fear*. I know the *fear* will taunt me always, but your words as testimony in past tense will be part of my memory bank, holding me steady in my *now-fear*. I can already see how these words *will grow me*!

• • • • • •

Holding the letter in my hand, I rushed to my file and pulled out my essay that concludes,

Grateful am I for the times I asked for light and He gave me the dark. For it was there, helpless, frightened, completely dependent, I realized my own inadequacies and my deep *need* of God. I wanted to know and see! But He knew that in the dark I would learn lessons that would escape me in the busyness and fulfillment of light.

I offer my thanks for the wishes I hung upon golden stars that I might find ease and laughter and companionship, which hung there all unfulfilled as I walked a rocky path with tears on my cheeks and felt the sting of loneliness. But it was on that path that I found Christ in a deeper, richer way than ever before. And a troubled heart found serenity and a seeking soul found guidance. I wanted only joy. But He left that wish on a scampering star and gave me sorrow, which enriched my life.

> *I thank you, Lord, for answered prayer,*
> *and for thy gifts that glow;*
> *But to my foolish longings, Lord,*
> *thank you for saying, "No!"*
> *I am so grateful for thy light,*
> *and all the joys I know;*
> *But to my selfish prayers, O Lord,*
> *thank you for saying, "No!"*

I bowed my head in that holy moment to whisper this young man's brave teenage prayer. . . . I prayed for him . . . I prayed for me: "O God, please let your love *grow us!*"

· · · · · ·

Oh, how I do love my own Anita, trembling in the night!

Thanks for letting me share your night of terror. I've prayed about how to answer your vitally important letter.

I guess I'll begin with a quote from a psychology book I read in college: "Fear is the most powerful emotion, second only to love." I branded that phrase on my brain, for I knew that in my life it was true.

My precious child, I've always known about fear.

Let me explain in chronology. One of my earliest memories is sitting on the cement steps in front of our parsonage understanding that I lived in a family of perfect giants. In my view of the world, my parents, my siblings—much older than I—were achieving, strong, wonderful, perfect giants! And I hugged my small self in my arms, rocking in self-comfort, clearly understanding I was only a plain, ordinary, quiet little girl.

I remember how I shuddered in fear that these perfect giants might ultimately find me out . . . and know. I could never be wonderful like they! And I wondered, would they disown me? Would they drown me? They were kind, loving, but their own wonders terrified me. There was no rational reason for any of this. I can only tell you that my child-mind knew fear.

My mother's favorite adjective for admirable people was "outstanding." While in college, my brothers each won the honor of being named the *Who's Who in American Colleges Outstanding Senior Boy.* Their achievements made me proud, happy to be their little sister . . . but where could I ever fit in to this perfect family of achievers? I examined myself closely. I could find only a plain, ordinary, quiet little girl.

As I grew, it became obvious to those looking on that I was neither ordinary *nor* quiet! But that was on the outside, where talents and dynamism dazzled. . . . Inside, there came another fear. When I was a high school senior, I was given a scholarship as "The Outstanding Senior Girl." Basking in all the verbal jubilance of my perfect giants, who most admired "outstanding" people, I danced joyfully to their happy melodies. But in the night I wondered if they really knew that the "plain, ordinary, quiet little girl" existed. This was Olive Ruth Wood. Would they love her *without* the talent, the dynamism? As I became Ruth Wood the overachiever, there was always an inner fear.

As I grew into maturity, there were enough life experiences for me to know the fear was real. People came to bask in my glory . . . but when there was no glory, I felt alone. Oh, Anita, of course I was unfair in my judgments! I have proven that my parents, my siblings, and many friends indeed knew and loved the plain, ordinary, quiet Olive Ruth with fervent loyalty. But, sad as it is, it took decades for *me* to know!

This is my honest response to your sharing your fears.

I have always known fear. Fear is universal, but I don't believe this specific fear beginning in childhood is universal. As I understand my husband's growing-up years, he didn't know the fear of being unacceptable on the horizontal level. His parents were not professionals; his siblings were close to him in age. His brothers, though older, were not that different from the younger Bobby.

Each family is unique; each child's response to his family and environment is unique. This remains the universal: Fear is the most powerful emotion, second only to love. Bob and all of us earthlings have specific fears. I am only sharing what I know—an important *why* of the *who* of Ruth.

As the years passed and my beloved carousels exploded—many without a moment's notice—I often responded like the small child on the cement step, hugging myself in my own arms. And the childhood fear accelerated into unadulterated terror. Oh yes, I understand every syllable of your letter.

Anita, this is true: There have been times in my adult life when I have held myself together in my own arms as my heart thundered in frightened panic. There have been times in my life when *all* I had known, trusted, and loved blew up in a moment of time and I sat in the ashes of my world, rocking like the child on the cement step.

I, too, knew the verse "Perfect love casteth out fear." I, too, should have allowed perfect love to cast out fear. I was an adult! I should have let my head knowledge translate into heart knowledge. But, Anita, you're right! Too often, it made no difference that my head knew Jesus said, "Be not afraid; it is I!" . . . or my translation: "Don't be scared, Ruth; I'm here!" I could whisper those words, but it was my own voice and I knew it.

I couldn't see Him. I couldn't hear Him. I couldn't touch Him. As a child once said, I needed "a God with skin on"! And He was not there.

Finally there came a day when I moved from the ash heap of my most beloved carousel to the computer. I knew I must deal with *fear*. For a lifetime I had known the neat, tidy answer. But I had never known what the words meant: "Perfect love casteth out fear!"

Let me share my journal record with you.

> I must, *I must* understand these five words. What do they mean? To me?
>
> Well, of course, Jesus *is* Perfect Love and He proved that when He gave himself for me, even in crucifixion. If I believe that, then even when I face pain, injustice, betrayal . . . watch beloved carousels blazing . . . I can know that I *can* live through all losses triumphantly. There *can* be new carousels of beauty.
>
> Why do I write this? Because I believe that Jesus lived *through* Calvary!
>
> Ruth, think clearly: Jesus was no ethical hero testing his soul and endurance on that cross. He was the Son of God testifying in His human nature to deepest human misery . . . and in His divine nature testifying that God, the Father of all mankind, loves His creation in its deepest misery. (End of that journal entry.)
>
> I'm back. It's been days as I've tried to think through Perfect Love. I shrink from clichés and I have never examined the cross beyond cliché! After a lifetime of Easters, I'm ashamed to admit it, but there it is!
>
> Now it occurs to me that the cross on which Jesus died affects me here and now and can heal the *fear* that attacks the marrowbone of my spirit. That *is* where the pain lies, of course. I have worked out so much in my mind, but I have discovered

that what the mind knows does not seem to exercise much influence on the way I really live!

That's shocking, Ruth, but true! Try to think *clearly*!

The mind does not usually control the spirit because, in spite of all my head knowledge, my spirit continues in its fear, which threatens to drown me. I find I cannot really believe in Perfect Love. Why? Because as a God identity, as a synonym for God's own name . . . I know I am so unworthy of Perfect Love companioning me because I know I never, ever live completely by the eternal laws of love in my humanity. Why? *Because I cannot!* Because I am so *imperfect*, somehow it's hard to accept *Perfect Love* as a synonym for the name of the personality I call God. Scares me.

I don't know why it's so hard, so scary . . . except in all my frailties, fallibilities, failures . . . why *is* it logical to have faith in God's perfect love for me, the small me?. . . (Think, Ruth, think carefully!). . . To have faith *is* illogical . . . except that on the cross, the God of perfect love, the God who *is* Perfect Love, the God whose name is Perfect Love said:

> *Here is my proof of forgiveness*
> *for your human frailties,*
> *your human fallibilities,*
> *your human failures.*
> *Here is my proof of accepting you,*
> *understanding you,*
> *participating WITH you,*
> *IN you, every moment.*
> *On Calvary's cross,*
> *you see my proof of constant,*
> *companioning Perfect Love.*
> *All you have to do is believe.*
> *The opposite of sin and fear*
> *is no longer virtue;*

it is faith:
faith in my perfect love for you
shown here in the broken body of my Son.
Here is my guarantee
of an unwavering relationship forever
between Father and child.

Is this what the Cross means?

The Old Testament is filled with wonderful exploits between Father and child, but only for moments, always episodic! Nothing ever lasted. When Moses came down from the mountain with the tablet of stone, the skin of his face glowed because He had been talking directly with God. But skin-glow of divine flame faded! The bright light of Oneness darkened. As always, there was the slow dissolving, the glow-setting, the floating-down . . . down . . . down . . . into only the memory of God talking, communing, being with man . . . that was true, Ruth, until . . . until . . . until . . .

Is this what the Cross means?

. . . until God put His whole self into human embryo and a baby was born of woman, grew, lived among us, until His flesh was torn and His blood shed for us . . . all of us, even me . . . until . . . until . . . until . . .

Is this what the Cross means?
O God, help me to think clearly. . . .

. . . until . . . until . . . talking with you was no longer a matter of climbing a mountain to you as did Moses, but a matter of Jesus, the divine Son of God, *descending to us* . . . until . . . God conversed with humanity *in* His Son and *on* the cross and would forevermore . . .

even now . . . twentieth century . . .
even now . . . broken life: Olive Ruth Wood . . .
Even now.

That is perfect love.
Right? Right.

"Perfect love casteth out fear."

And when I am no longer afraid of the unknown smashing my life to bits, reducing all my successes into total failures, I am able to be free. And *love, as I have studied for a lifetime, is always the other side of the same coin with freedom* . . . for perfect love is free love that has no strings attached . . . no conditions that say, "When you are safe in the security of beloved family relationships . . . when life runs on normal . . . when you are healthy, brilliant, dynamic, and achieving, Ruth, I will love you." *No!* No required conditions.

The vertical relationship with divine personality assures me that *He is Perfect Love* and, if I will allow, He will "cast out *fear*"—fear of my losses, of life changes, of my feelings of unacceptability on the horizontal plane.

This I claim: If I truly believe and understand the significance of what Jesus did on the cross, *He has proven He is Perfect Love* to me on the vertical plane, and in that proof, I can open myself to His power to cast out *all* fear!—of broken dreams, human aloneness, physical disabilities, and all of the other unknown, unwanted, unpleasant circumstances of human life . . . for . . .

> *in this moment*
> *I choose to believe with unswerving certainty*
> *that the action of the Son of God on the Cross*
> *says to me authoritatively:*
> *Ruth, you are loved.*
> *Period.*
> *End of that discussion.*

Perfect Love says on the cross, "Ruth, you are loved. What is your response to me?"

And there I am left with a personal choice.

I am not the victim here. I keep wanting to be the victim. It's so comfortable to be the victim. But if I *choose* to companion *Perfect Love* as dynamic ever-present Personality, then I am *free* from all torture points that come on the horizontal plane! I am free only when I choose to open myself to His working in me, for me, through me . . .

> *and when I choose . . . I do not need to be afraid*
> *for I am never, ever alone!*
> *When I know He is with me, in me, I can prove*
> *He, who is Perfect Love, is Redeemer. . .*
> *of all humanly frightening, heartbreaking circumstance!*
> *My God will make creative use of every carousel sliver, every dream*
> *splatter, every salty tear.*

A holy hush descends just now and I find myself whispering the old hymn, "Just as I am without one plea, except thy blood was shed for me . . . I come. I come."

Anita, this journal record is my best answer to human fear, no matter the catalyst: *Perfect love casteth out fear.*

I am grateful this is not a command. I cannot obey, no matter how much I may wish to!

The Good News is that Perfect Love understood this was not relevant for commands. *This is a declarative statement of what is available* when the human mind can understand the word meanings and can be brave enough to *choose to allow Perfect Love to cast out all fear!* In all of life's seasons. One need never be afraid. Oh, Anita, *it is a choice!*

As I, age sixty, sit at the computer today, writing to you in your fortieth year, tears stream down my cheeks, my heart bulges in throbbing gratitude, and with determined courage, I whisper, "O Lamb of God, O Perfect Love, I come . . . I come . . . I come . . . from the known past into the unknown future, all unafraid . . . I come because I know you are *with me.* You are *Perfect Love.*"

I conclude this letter in holy hush, praying this may help you in your own life fears—known, unknown, present, and future—for I do believe in these words: *You find the answer . . . if you choose.*

I understand every syllable of your letter, Anita. I can only pray with all my love that you can come to find His peace available. His peace will never be instantaneous or constant. I know. Fear still can grab me like a dog with a rabbit, leaving me helpless, powerless, frantic . . . until I choose to remember Perfect Love . . . and then *choose to face life with Him in me, with me, for me.* Then peace comes.

Oh, my beloved child, learn to be quicker than I am in choosing.

Here is my prayer . . . for us both. . . .

—Moddy

Facing Relationships With Others at Forty

ANITA HIGMAN

Yes, sitting around the table during the holidays . . . what a joy-ride of sweet splendor. And oh, how dangerous that joyride can be to family relationships! Somewhere between the sweet potatoes and our splendorous intentions, words get crossed and there go our relationships, careening near the edge of extinction.

"What did I say, hon? How could he have misunderstood me? I only meant that I would try to be extra sensitive to his inflexible behavior. I want to be giving to him in that way. How could he be offended by my generous attitude?"

Perhaps misunderstandings will grow thinner as I get older. But it seems the only thing that is getting thinner is my husband's hair.

"What did I say, hon? You know I love your hair that way. It has so much more room to breathe now that there is so much less of it."

I wonder if Moddy can rescue me from my own "good" intentions.

· · · · · ·

DEAR MODDY,

I want you to know that when everything in our universe seems to be spiraling out of control, there are two constants in this life:

God is and *Ruth Vaughn is out there somewhere celebrating life.*

The reason I say this is because *that* is what you do best. And usually your daily life banquet also offers an effervescent toast not only to your friends but to all those people fortunate enough to cross your path. Honestly, that is truly how I see you. You love without question, without judging, and without ever demanding its return.

While most people are feeling disconnected and stressed out and sliding down all sorts of slippery slopes, you are busily dusting them all with joy. Once I wrote, "When you have a generous heart, joy is only a kind deed away." That makes me think of you, Moddy. I would love to live like that.

I would like people not so much to wonder who I am, but to know they have seen Jesus in what I have done. I know that isn't easy. I dream of emanating Him in all my relationships. And then something usually goes wrong.

People have this nasty habit of being too human. I try to give, and they don't always want. I try to love, and they shrug their shoulders. I try to be a joy sparkler in their lives, and they seem to find pleasure in spitting on my little light and watching it sputter out.

I remember a friendship years ago with a man I worked with. No matter how upbeat I tried to be, he was negative. I tried to be pleasant, but he tended to reply with biting remarks. He always laughed a lot to take the edge off the insult. But it hurt just the same. That friendship died very quickly. Another friendship I recall started out well, but ended with misunderstanding, confusion, and pain.

You know, Moddy, I honestly thought my relationships with people would be different at forty. Easier. But poor communication and conflict and judgment and envy and testy attitudes still rear their ugly heads from time to time.

And those not-so-pleasant elements of human character thrive in families too. My husband and I have a good relationship, but it could be better. My children and I adore one another, but I know I could be a better mother. I am close to them all now, but I worry sometimes if we will grow apart. Then I will wonder if I should have listened more. Should I have laughed more? Should I have been less critical? Could I have loved more? There are some days that I feel I have failed them all. We are still a good, healthy family in many ways, but I believe I could be and do more.

In other relationships, people seem to like me for the most part, but sometimes I think I am not terribly easy to get along with. Sometimes, without much warning, I can get sucked into the undertow of bad attitudes.

In fact, it seems America in general has felt the pull of these frightening waters. People aren't as kind as they used to be. They seem to be edgier, less courteous, less trusting, and less gentle with each other. I hate what I see happening, and then I look in the mirror. To my horror, when I look deeply, I know in my heart that I have been guilty of it too.

I write good stuff in my journal, Moddy, but I'm afraid I don't live it much. But here's something else I wrote: "A brief shower of good deeds nourishes the spirit better than a flood of good intentions." See what I mean? Maybe that's what I give too much of . . . merely good intentions.

I know while 1 Corinthians 13 has been recited at many weddings for a nice ceremonial touch, you, Moddy, are out there living it! It's so lovely to read, but sometimes so unlovely when I try to play it out on the stage of humanity.

I guess if I were to boil this letter down into two questions, they would be, "What is your philosophy of relationships with other people?" and "What makes you behave the way you do?"

Thanks for allowing me to write you anything, anytime. You are truly a dear, Moddy. And I promise I am honestly trying to do more than file your letters away in a pretty box. I'm really working at folding your wisdom into my heart and into the creases of my daily life. It can happen! In fact, many things are already happening deep inside of me this fortieth year. Things that wouldn't have happened if we had not reached across space after years of separation to discover that the heart-bond we knew during my college years has remained. This is more precious to me than words can say.

It's such a wonder, Moddy, really! When we finally met again, it was as if we'd never been apart. The love has remained. You've kept my picture on your wall all these years, and I never knew. I'm afraid I don't follow through with relationships as I should.

I left college, still a kid, and spent all my time building my own carousel. It's not that I forgot the carousel I whirled in laughing magic with you; it's just that I rushed on to create my own carousel. That's okay, of course, but I wish I'd had enough sense to always be a part of the unique relationship you've allowed me. Billy and Ronnie are now adult professionals. They still call you Moddy. I'm so glad I can be an "adopted daughter" and also use their pet lovename. Do know. . .

—Anita loves Moddy!

Identification Is the Key

RUTH VAUGHN

Today my schedule was written out. I knew "the miles I must go, the promises I must keep before I sleep," to quote Robert Frost.

All of a sudden, there was the strong impression that my schedule needed to be adjusted and my first task was to go to the home of a friend. I really prayed about it! I was overcommitted on this day. I had talked to Jenny yesterday in happy, busy chatter with my joyful congratulations on a new promotion she had received. I had *no* time to rush off to see her this morning. There was no reason to see her today, yet the impression would not budge.

So, assuming I was being silly, I swooshed down the freeway to her home to see if the impression might be from God. When she opened the door, she sighed deeply and whispered, "Please come in."

We went to the table, and I looked at her carefully. There was a look of tidied-up despair burning in her eyes. I had not taken the time to notice her eyes the day before. Now I touched her hand. "Is there anything I can do?" There was no cry of response; just a sigh. And then the low burning shot into a flame. "You came! I hoped so long. I don't need anything. It's here where the trouble is." Her hand moved to her heart.

And there in her kitchen, we moved easily into each other's inner souls—perceiving, caring, sharing . . . giving, learning, and loving. *The Father guided us that day.*

So often when I share another's success and joy, that is all I notice. I don't look deeper; I don't look closely enough. But when I do, there is often a longing in their eyes, and I wonder if they're saying—

as I have said—"I'm here. Inside. Please find me! Not the success, not the outer facade, the *inner* me! Oh, please, tell me I'm worthwhile. Tell me you are my friend and you care about me, the person."

We are God's children. We belong together.

· · · · · ·

I come to the computer laughing at the end of your last letter! So I'll begin like this:

· · · · · ·

MODDY LOVES ANITA!

Well, I reread your questions: "What is your philosophy of relationships with other people?" and "What makes you behave the way you do?"

Oh, my child, I can only give you the answer I heard my mother give all the years of my growing up. It is a poem. (I have no idea where she found it or who wrote it.) I can only tell you she chose its words to form her relationships with others . . . and, of course, in her living example, its lines became a part of my very being. Here it is:

If I could only see the road you came,
The jagged rocks and crooked ways,
I would more kindly think of your misstep
And only praise.

If I could know the heartaches you have felt,
The longings for the things that never came,
I would not harshly judge your erring then
Nor even blame.

I could end my response to your letter now, Anita. This is such a vital key, I believe, to all relationships in life. You learned the noun for this in your college English class: *identification*. It is also representative of the old Indian proverb: "Never judge a person until you have walked two miles in his moccasins."

In my life, there are many "moccasins" I have never worn. And I never will. But I can choose to care deeply about each person I meet. No matter the moccasins they wear.

Anita, I often wonder when Jesus said, "Love one another," if, indeed, He did not mean, "Listen to one another." I know I can never, ever love another person unless I first *listen* to that person! The more I listen, the more I understand some of the *whys* that make another's *who* so different from my own! In careful, perceptive listening, Anita, I can love as Jesus loved.

You spoke of your colleague who was always negative, never responding to your laughing, friendly overtures. I remember an elderly church janitor who served when I was in charge of the youth program. After each party, I would enthusiastically thank him for his efforts, often kissing his cheek. He would brush me away: "No sense in those kids making such a mess!" But in his eyes, Anita, I knew he loved what I was doing with those kids who were "making such a mess!"

Shakespeare said it: "Love gives a precious seeing to the eye." That janitor's gruffness, his brushing me away, didn't fool me. He might not have responded the way I had wished. He would never laugh at my nonsense, but later I would often find him grinning. "If I could only know the road he came" . . . then I would love with understanding, but since he never shared the specifics, I could only love what I knew of him, regardless of his reaction to me.

A second important key also comes from my mother. She chose to articulate her philosophy by singing a poem written by the blind poet Fanny Crosby, which was set to music years ago. It is the old hymn "Rescue the Perishing." Here is one stanza:

Down in the human heart,
crushed by the tempter,
Feelings lie buried
that grace can restore;
Touched by a loving heart,
wakened by kindness,
Chords that are broken
will vibrate once more.

Mother sang those words around the house almost daily. And most vital in my growing-up years were the object lessons of those words that I observed. The most unlovely people came to our parsonage, often leaving the entire atmosphere stinking with dark, foul alcohol fumes and cigarette smoke. Sometimes they would be so drunk, they vomited all over her clean floor. And Mother loved them through it all. When they were cleaned up and left the house, my mother would sit me down and gently quote to me Fanny Crosby's words. Of course, the words became the very fabric of my being. *Chords that are broken will vibrate once more.*

I believed them as a child because I could observe their truth. For hours, my parents listened to the most angry, rebellious, vile people . . . believing that inside the dreadful-smelling exterior, *Feelings [lay] buried that grace [could] restore!* I observed those "untouchables" touched by my parents' loving hearts . . . blinking from sin/fear/blindness and *wakened by kindness* . . . and some of them responded so fully that *Chords that [were] broken [would] vibrate once more.* Some are most beautifully vibrating today . . . even throughout the world!

Oh, if there were time, I could tell you stories of several hundred hopeless lives who, to this day, are joyful Christians because my parents followed Fanny Crosby's challenge! Some are successful ministers of music, ministers of Christian education; some are behind the pulpit preaching the *grace* given to them *first* in a parsonage where they were accepted, loved, cherished . . . even when they were the most unlovely!

I saw it. I lived it. And as I grew to maturity, I was the one meeting people in these most desperate conditions, and I was able to give them unconditional love . . . trying, as I observed my parents before me, to follow in Jesus' steps of acceptance, understanding, non-judgmental care, intercessory prayer, and vibrant faith, *knowing* the beauty these broken lives could become . . . if they would choose to accept the gift of His grace. Of course, many moved right along on their chosen life roads in spite of any love or help I might offer them. I have sat with some at the crossroads and said, "I know you have chosen this road of your own making. I accept that, but if you ever decide you would like to change roads and follow God, *please let me be the one to hold your hand and help you find your way."* And some did. I have personally observed the miracle of hearts that were broken vibrating once more!

Jesus is merciful; Jesus will save.

In this letter response, Anita, I would add one other small poem that has become vital in my philosophy of relationships with others. It was written by Edwin Markham:

He drew a circle that shut me out.
Heretic, rebel, a thing to flout.
But love and I had the wit to win,
We drew a circle that took him in.

This is the third major key in my philosophy of relationships with others. I have found this truth: No matter how others may reject me, *love and I* can choose to love them and include them. I can choose to give love freely. My love may be rejected or accepted. The person may have moved or grown beyond my reach. But whatever, wherever . . . my heart faithfully loves . . . even across space.

When my sons, Billy and Ronnie, each graduated from high school, I wrote a book celebrating their birth, their growth, and their independence to move autonomously away from home. To Ron, in a scary time in his growing life, I wrote,

If I could
I would croon reality away
With cradle songs . . .
We would gently rock
And weep bewilderment
Together. . .
But . . .
You are beyond my reach.
His trust must be
Your shield and buckler.

It's just you
And the "Most High"
Together now.

No mommies allowed.

. . . except in loving "prayer without ceasing" for the beloved child.

When each of my sons was born, I began to fill shoe boxes with all my letters to them, poetry about them, prayers for them, along with photographs and *all* memorabilia pertaining to their lives as they grew to become high school seniors. Each of their senior years, I took a week aside, pulled all these materials together, and formed them into a coherent book. Each was bound in red leather with gold engraving: Billy Edward. Ronald Charles.

These are very different books because my sons are very different boys with very different life experiences, even though they are brothers who grew up with the same parents in the same home. There is only one page that is identical. It is the last:

Tall young stranger
On the move,
Child I used to know . . .
Here's a token as you pass . . .
In its magic, go
Where you will.
You can never be lost.
It is your Come-Back Key:
I'll always love you.

Of course, my love for these two young men is different from any other because they are my own flesh and blood. My love for them is fiercely fervent in a unique dimension . . . and they know it! One talked to me on the phone this week. As we were concluding the conversation, I said, "I love you," and he responded, "I have never doubted it for a millisecond!"

But, Anita, although in a different way from Billy and Ronnie, there is no person in my realm of acquaintance to whom I do not give the "Come-Back Key" of unconditional love anytime, anywhere, when that one chooses to accept it. Some have rejected me and walked away. That is their privilege. As it is my privilege to continue to love them.

You, my child, have chosen to love me, cherish me, allow me to be a vital part of your life. I can whisper the same words to you that I wrote for my sons, for I knew you as an eighteen-year-old child *on the move.* . . . I was your professor and I did my best to be a good academician those learning years. But of greater importance, I loved you with a maternal love. Although you were not my birth child, you also knew the depth of my love and grew in its warmth.

I am grateful. I rejoice. We grow together.

But those who have drawn a circle to shut me out cannot diminish me. Because love and I can draw a circle to bring that person in. Any person, any time, can choose to reject, to walk away. In the same freedom, I can choose to continue to love, no matter where the person is or what that person does or leaves undone. My love remains available only for the asking. This is my choice and no one can take it from me.

So . . . I have read your letter over and over, Anita. I find that in these three *keys* you can read the whole of my life philosophy in relating to others. I give them to you for your own consideration. Please know these thoughts are enveloped with all my loving prayers. . . .

—Moddy

c h a p t e r 11 *e l e v e n*

Exploring a Body Changing at Forty

ANITA HIGMAN

Some days I get up and my forty-year-old body says, "Good morning, little bluebird."

Other mornings my body says, "You mean, I'm expected to get up today too?"

I feel a change coming down the line. I wonder if it's the menopause locomotive. If it is, I want off! I didn't buy a ticket, and I don't like where it's going.

Stop this thing. I want off!!

I never thought the word "derailment" would look so good.

. . . . . .

MY MODDY DEAR,

Guess what now?

Well, now it's the *M* word.

And I don't mean Moddy. I mean menopause.

What is this thing? People talk about it like it's a fiery meteor ready to hit all earth women who are middle-aged. (Although that would explain hot flashes.) Anyway, I am wondering if this flaming ball is headed straight for me!

Menopause . . . the change of life. Awesome sounding, isn't it? Like some ominous and ethereal pause in our lives when we are hit with all of life's wisdom, and elder womanhood is ours for the taking. That's fine. I'll take it, as long as I can be twenty while I'm doing it. But no cigar. I am trapped in a forty-year-old body. And it's ticking. I mean, I am glad I'm still ticking, but sometimes it seems like the ticking reminds me of a bomb rather than a gift of more time on this planet.

In my thesaurus there are listed a zillion different phobias. I hope I'm not coming down with menopause and forty-phobia, if there is such a thing.

As far as the *M* word is concerned, I am becoming more tired and irritable with miserable mood swings. Also my periods are changing, I'm gaining weight, and I seem to sweat like a beast.

The other day I was at a church function. I perspired so much the odor became embarrassing. I fled to the ladies' room in an effort to dry off. I took my facial powder from my compact and dabbed it frantically under my armpits with a paper towel. Later I emerged with my weapons covered, making no sudden movements, so as not to asphyxiate my comrades. In other words, I think perspiring is becoming a real problem. And I can't help but wonder if all this "stuff" in my life means I am on the verge of menopause.

And, as I mentioned before about growing older in general, I'm not throwing any "Happy Aging" parties for myself. The other day I was holding my two kids in our big recliner, and they both started noticing my hands. They said something like, "Why are your veins bulging out like that on your hands? They look funny." Well, I love the honesty of my kids, but sometimes reality is not a pretty sight. It is instead grotesquely comical. Like my purple spider veins, my dye-defying gray hairs, and my toenails that resemble something thrown in a brew along with eye-of-newt.

But then all of what I say, I suppose, should take into consideration my temperament. I am a melancholic, so I specialize in the fearful, the morbid, and the depressing. Melancholics have very positive qualities, too, but these listed are some of what I call "the dark rushes" in our lives.

So I figure the way I age and the way I feel about my aging will be affected by my temperament. Don't you think?

For one thing, at forty, I feel thick. In my spirit, in my body, and in my emotions. Even my thighs and parts of my thinking feel thick.

And my cackler is showing again. The chicken is back. I am kind of spooked about this change-of-life thing. I have heard some stories about women who didn't have a ball with it . . . *at all*. It was more like becoming one of the ugly stepsisters for a while, or getting bloated up into a coach and forced to ride frantically through the night.

I remember another crazy ride. When I went into labor with my first child. Once the birthing process was steamrolling along, I became frightened. I knew this was IT. I couldn't stop for a coffee break. It wouldn't do any good to claim squeamishness and leave the travail behind, because the travail followed me everywhere. Childbearing felt like some sick magician's nightmare as I writhed in a painful body trap, unable to escape. And then there is this audience of miscellaneous people who gather in your room to watch the show. I began to wonder if they were going to set up a stand and sell popcorn and hot dogs.

Anyway, giving birth was absolutely worth it all, because I love my children deeply. *But*, at the time, it surely makes a woman want to scream, "Get me out of this!! I'll slip you a thousand-dollar bonus if you'll do a C-section *now*!!"

My point is, if this is indeed menopause for me, I just hope I don't start getting that same kind of panic like I had when I was in labor. Because it has that same funny smell to it—like that pungent dirt odor right before you're buried alive in a mudslide. I mean, having my periods slow down to nothing sounds like the tunnel of glories, yet it's really just another strange passageway we women are expected to squeeze through with our bellies sucked in and our smiles at attention. Well, this is one female earth camper who's burned her panty girdle and donned the drama mask of tragedy.

I guess I'll leave you with my usual upbeat closing! Sorry!

Besides my ranting and raving, Moddy, I do have some solid questions about my changing body.

Do you think I should be having regular physicals? Did you have a plan of action when you reached this time of life? When did you go through menopause? Was it tough, or did you fly through it wondering what the fuss was about?

Thanks again, Moddy, for listening to my crazies.

Love from someone who's wondering if she's about to sprout gorilla hair on her chin and sing the "Menopause Blues"!

—Anita

Take Care of It!

RUTH VAUGHN

She knew I was coming. At that time.

I rang the doorbell and heard Shelley yell, "If it's Ruth, come in. If not, do not, I repeat, do *not* enter until I invite you!"

I opened the door and entered the house. The kitchen was directly on the right, and so as I stepped into the foyer, I gasped at the most shocking sight. My friend had placed her head on the top shelf of the refrigerator, both arms lying on a lower shelf! This adult, mature woman was literally *in* her refrigerator.

"Shelley, what on earth are you doing?"

"Trying to breathe through this hot flash!"

I laughed till I cried. But it was not funny. We both knew it wasn't, but the sight of the long-discussed "change of life" was too vividly hilarious for me to respond differently. It *was* funny!

When the hot flash passed and she could close the refrigerator door, Shelley and I talked long and seriously about this female phenomenon. It is very real and very uncomfortable. We women don't like it, but *there it is*!

This is a true story. Shelley allowed me to enclose this anecdote here but wanted the assurance that I would change her name. *The woman in the refrigerator is definitely anonymous!*

· · · · · ·

OH, MY DEAR GORILLA-HAIRED BLUES SINGER,

How you do make me laugh! Easy to see why you enchanted me the first moment we met! You are my pure delight!

I'm glad you wrote the letter in your hilarious fashion. For in all the silliness, there was serious importance. Oh, my Anita, I'm so proud of you. Instead of trying to slough it off, you, at forty, perceive it is wise to stop and assess *where you are* in time and *how you are* in terms of your body's structure and function. As these letters have stressed, you are now in the prime of your life. Of that, you can be sure. In spite of the sweats and your concern for losing all your friends with your odor! Anita, you are *so funny*! What a wonderful gift God has given to our world with your unique "way with words." Inimitable, you are.

But . . . it *is indeed* natural to feel sadness that youth is behind you, to feel nostalgia for the enthusiasm of your twenties, to feel fear, betrayal, and anger at a body changing. Not at your request!! Accept all of those normal, natural feelings, Anita; know the losses, mourn them, scream loudly if you need to . . . and then sit quietly and ponder the question that seemed so silly in the bathroom when you were drying your odoriferous body! Come, think with me. Can there not be a way to find excitement in exploring Browning's line, "The last of life, for which the first was made"?

In light of your letter's eloquent description, I know the poetry sounds pretty silly. But still consider the possibility of finding the adventure. I know. I'm sitting coolly in my home, while you may be at a party shrieking in hot flashes. Easy for me to philosophize. I know anything I say may sound pretty dumb.

But let me try, even if you do want to turn me off! Here are the facts we both know: Your body has changed from childhood to puberty to full womanhood. Including periods and childbirth. Okay. Done that. Got the T-shirt. But now your body's going to change again! Body changes in your past have been dramatic; they seem on a dramatic course toward the future. Have you been to see your gynecologist (GYN)? With today's medical technology, it is most probable you will come through this unscathed.

Of course, you understand the obvious: To live these next forty years to their fullest, you need to be in the best physical health possible as you, at forty, face a body changing. Do I advise a physical?

You know I have counseled women for decades. I always plead that in this fortieth year, a woman ask for a medical evaluation with a complete physical. I urge you: *Do it now!* And make it an annual practice.

Anita, as you face the Big *M*—menopause—I would suggest you study another classic book written by Gail Sheehy. Entitled *The Silent Passage*, she presents a fact-filled discussion of this changing of a woman's body. Filled with anecdotes, it is compelling reading, and I believe you will find it invaluable to have in your library.

I'm little help on the subject. Because of Addison's disease, I was placed on estrogen supplements decades ago. And, in the uniqueness of my body, I never had a problem. Menopause was over before I knew it began. To me, it was nothing, but for one of my close friends, menopause threw her into a total personality change. She became a hot, sweating, unhappy, distressed, yelling emotional wreck, and we, who loved her, wondered if she would ever find *herself* again. It took years, but she "came back" as the darling we used to know. But she is much older than I! She would tell you that she believes current medical science could have prevented, certainly decelerated, the horrors she endured.

In these examples, I share my knowledge of the two extremes. But, Anita, I urge you to read Gail Sheehy's book so you can prepare knowledgeably for this powerful body change normal in all females. With the medical technology today, it has to be more pleasant than in days past.

Yes, my dear, I know you are a "big cackler chicken" and never want to go a doctor! Never! But listen to me carefully as I plead for you to go to your primary doctor for a complete physical of all elements of your body. *Now.* My primary doctor, an endocrinologist because of my Addison's disease, calls it "a total survey of the body."

If you do this, Anita, he or she, of course, will include your GYN "survey" of all the female elements and suggest how best to prepare for menopause, free of fear. I'm sure you are already having regular mammograms and pap smears? Please take these seriously, Anita. My grandfather and my aunt both died of cancer. I have had two pap smears that alerted my gynecologist to the beginnings of cancer. Caught so quickly, the tumors could be quickly, easily removed. No matter how busy your schedule, make these two tests a priority! As I'm sure you know, when detected early, there is no reason for your female organs to cause a major problem.

Now, there is a second thing I always advise a woman at age forty. Begin to research your family health history—generations back.

I know my physical history is unique, but I'll share the things I think might be a bit helpful. In my thirty-ninth year, my longtime physician was sending me to every specialist to try to discover *the* diagnosis of my continued weight loss and total fatigue. He made an appointment for me to have a work-up by a gynecologist of his choice. When the nurse called to confirm my appointment, she told me to bring along a family health history, *using as many generations as possible.*

Anita, I was astonished. The nurse assured me that learning as much as possible about my family health history is probably *the* single most important preventive step we can take against ill health and disease approaching forty. I asked her why. She explained that I may have inherited genes from my family tree that make me more apt to develop certain illnesses. These can be prevented or attenuated if, knowing about them early enough, a woman can change her diet or lifestyle or avoid certain precipitating factors.

I found the assignment daunting. Neither my grandparents nor my parents were available for this kind of information. I had never thought of a family-tree health history in my life. I wasn't terribly helpful in this area, because all I knew of my paternal grandparents were the facts that he died of cancer and my grandmother died of tuberculosis, as did one of her sons and two of her grandsons. My maternal grandparents were seen only a few times in my life; my grandfather broke his hip and died with complications when I was seven. I went to my grandmother's funeral but assumed she had died of old age. My mother's illness had never been definitively diagnosed, and she lay in a coma the last thirteen months of her life. No one seemed to have a clue as to exactly *why*. My father was vibrantly strong, preached his last sermon on his ninetieth birthday, and died of a heart attack a few weeks later.

The only physical problem I had ever known of my mother's was that she had developed two internal tumors on her uterus prior to my birth. She had worried they would affect me, but all seemed normal. Remember, this was in an era when doctors were rarely consulted. The one who agreed to come to our home for my birth said the tumors were no problem; they seemed benign. My mother hated them because they made her stomach bigger. The doctor chided her about her vanity! And that was that!

I had always been healthy and strong, with one exception. Since childhood, whenever my life activities demanded unusual amounts of energy, I fainted. One of the great embarrassments of my youth occurred during a college freshman play rehearsal: I fainted center stage. The infirmary told my parents it was exhaustion, and after a few days of complete bed rest, I was good as ever. And again, that was that! I learned to live with the dizziness, the unexpected weaknesses, the fainting, and moved on with vibrant life, with no concern other than the occasional embarrassment.

My medical history indicated that I had given birth to two sons. My other hospitalization was in a diagnostic hospital in 1966. The diagnosis eluded the doctor, although he gave me estrogen, which seemed to solve the problem. For the time.

Now my body was clutched in the grip of something that no one in Oklahoma City had been able to diagnose. So off I went to the gynecologist. The above account of my family health history is all I wrote because it was all I knew for sure. It was of little help to the GYN. All his tests and X-rays proved me fit in that area.

As you know, ultimately, I was sent to Scott and White Hospital, where the diagnostician was astute enough to put me into the endocrine ward, believing Addison's disease was moving me toward death. He had been correct.

In the jubilation of my return to life, he told me that the family health history had helped. I was amazed. He said, "Your mother's delivery of a child at the age of forty-four with two tumors pressing on the womb made me more careful to find a defect that could have been yours at birth. In that era, she probably had no prenatal care or advice. Your family history of tuberculosis alerted me to think of Addison's. It is my belief that you were born with a pituitary gland that was sluggish in its commands to the adrenals, hence the unexpected weakness, the fainting. As you grew older and lived under greater pressures, your body experienced pituitary overload and all commands to the adrenals finally ceased. As you explained, your last two years had been active by the most resolute willpower. You came here in the event of death. Your body's response to hydrocortisone, which is the best replacement medical science has found for atrophied adrenals, proves my diagnosis correct."

Even my skeletal family history saved my life.

That was the physical. To be most helpful, I believe you must include in a full family history, as well as *self-knowledge*, the emotional facets. This can be crucial.

Anita, recently, a young woman celebrated *her* fortieth birthday in my home. When it was all over, she sat with me alone, pulled off her party hat and threw it on the table, then presented me with a lengthy litany of physical problems. When she finished, she sighed deeply. "No doctor will take me seriously. They just tell me it's depression and I need a shrink!"

I, who know her well, understood her dilemma. All medical tests had proved normal, but approaching her fortieth birthday, she had gone into an emotional tailspin. She had quit her job, spending so much time in bed that she was concerned she was becoming agoraphobic. Coming to my home for a celebration had made her a frantic wreck. She had wanted to ask me to call it off that morning. "I would have . . . except you'd done all that work and people were coming. . . . Valium helped me through it . . . and I do appreciate it . . . the balloons, the laughter, the gifts . . . but I really would rather have been home in bed!"

Emotional health is vital for physical health, Anita. Perhaps the emotions are never more in play in the life of a woman than following her fortieth birthday. In this important "Silent Passage," as Gail Sheehy calls it, I find that women and many men develop a more acute need to assess the *whys* of the *who*. You know how much I have encouraged others to keep this self-discovery challenge constant. This search for self-knowledge, for inner peace, joy, and vibrancy, provides the foundation for your being your best physically!

Oh, my child, I'm telling you all this stuff because I so want to help you in the frustrated pain you wrote about in your last letter. You knew I would tell you to *know the why of your emotions . . . and of you*! Often it is in this period, when hormones go crazy, that pent up feelings erupt in the most amazing ways. I have spent many hours with my friend who was in such depression on her fortieth birthday. This is a time to go inward and understand the *why* of your emotions . . . but there is the very real physiological concern. I urge you to begin an in-depth generational health history. You can do better than I have done.

Consider it a fun challenge! It could be invaluable! A woman who took my challenge a few years ago worked out an extensive family medical tree. On it, the primary physician noted that her great-great-grandmother had died of colon cancer. No one else in the family tree had ever had cancer. This physician, however, demanded an annual physical because of this one instance of colon cancer. My friend hated it: drinking all that stuff in order to check the colon, when no other person in the family tree had a problem. But two years ago, cancer was detected. It was caught early enough that with surgery and chemotherapy she is today in vigorous health.

I know her well enough to know that if her physician had not insisted—because of her *great-great*-grandmother's colon cancer— she would have never, ever gone though the discomfort and indignities of that annual test. Following through on the knowledge of her great-great-grandmother's body may have saved my friend's life.

I could cite more examples of vital information coming from generations beyond one's parents. That's not necessary here. But do it for yourself . . . and develop one for Peter. Add those two documents to Scott and Hillary's family health histories of all childhood diseases, inoculations, and developmental problems they may have had since birth. In this way, you will be creating the most complete history possible. This will benefit Peter and could also assist Scott and Hillary . . . their children . . . their grandchildren.

Anita, I know your mother is not alive to help you in such a task, but I urge you to write all that you know of her health problems. You may even want to ask her primary physician to give you photocopied records. Go to Oklahoma, visit your family . . . or call, write your father, your brother, grandparents, aunts, uncles, any family members who may give a fuller record of your inherited genes.

With this information, Anita, your physician can better assist you when you go to him. Be as specific as you can. Record your own childhood diseases, inoculations, developmental problems, or any conditions you have had since birth. Next, list major illnesses and hospital stays. Since Addison's disease has been mine, I have understood the need to keep a careful record of hospital names, attending physicians, and specific diagnostic tests and procedures I underwent. Not only have my physicians called Dr. John Thompson, Scott and White Hospital, for information, but I have called him when I needed advice I felt that only he, in the unique capacity of being my attending physician at the time of diagnosis and my first adrenal-insufficiency crisis, could give me. I have been correct in each of those phone visits with the doctor who was *there with me.* Keep records not only of names but of places and phone numbers.

Anita, I just called my current GYN about writing this letter. She assured me that my family medical history had been important in her working with me in the last decade, but it was dreadfully incomplete. She told me that you should try to create a more comprehensive gynecological history at age forty than I had ever done. She said to begin with the date and body responses of your first onset of menstruation and any problems you may have experienced up to now. Record the methods of birth control you have used; if on the pill, indicate the brands taken.

"I don't anticipate she is near menopause yet," she said, "but in rare cases this can happen. If she has any menopausal symptoms, tell her to write careful notes." I didn't read your letter to her! But you might put the letter as part of your medical history! That would spice up all that boring stuff! Surprise your doctor, don't you agree?

Anita, my GYN surprised me just now by saying, "Tell her she also ought to write an occupational and social history. These can be valuable indicators of stress-related problems, to which so many illnesses and diseases seem to be linked today."

I knew this was vital! Had I ever shared with her, or any doctor, the pressure under which I worked in 1991, a near heart attack in my office might not have occurred. The cardiologist attending me at that time advised me to give up a full-time ghost writing job because of the intense stresses involved. I did. There have been no other heart problems! But I almost died that afternoon in my office. I had never dreamed occupational stress could affect the heart! My body proved it can! Big time!

But no doctor had ever given me the challenge to identify *occupational* or unusual *social stresses*. I do believe my GYN is exactly right. Occupational and social pressure information can be vital to a discerning physician.

And then my GYN said on the phone, "It would help a lot if Anita could be more specific than you have been in writing down ages, current health of parents, grandparents, brothers, sisters, other close relatives. If any of them are dead, the cause of death can be important. Heart disease, cancer, arthritis, diabetes, and hypertension are notorious for running in families. The further back in generational history she can go the better. If she cannot rely on memory alone, don't forget that most families usually have an old box stashed away somewhere in the attic that contains old newspaper clippings about family history, important events, birth certificates, and most importantly, death certificates. As morbid as it may sound, autopsy reports can carry an untold wealth of medical information that may reflect directly on one's own body." She paused, then said, "Tell her to start now, but keep it continually updated with any significant health changes in her life and in the lives of her relatives. Tell Anita to be more helpful in family history than you have been!" We laughed, chatted a bit, then I tried to write down her advice as closely as memory would allow.

As I read your letter with your concerns of your changing body, it seemed I might best help in this way. I can't address your specific concerns, for God created each of us uniquely. I have never had one female problem. I have never had a food allergy or any other specific problem you've experienced . . . just as you have never faced Addison's disease with its demands.

So . . . I'm answering your letter this way. Work on full understandings of the *who* and the *whys* for your unique body. For medical people, write the fullest family health history possible. Take it to your primary doctor and ask for a complete physical. If he finds your health perfect, then continue an annual exam so any undetected problems can be dealt with as soon as possible. Let medical science keep you constantly updated on the physical status of your changing body, Anita. Oh, do give the world the wonder of your finishing *your* last book on your 90th birthday . . . or with the constant medical technologies . . . maybe on your 190th!! And you are concerned about FORTY!!!

My dear "youngster," do know I send forever love and pray that you, too, will develop the capacity to be "forever young" in spirit. It is a choice.

—Moddy

Facing Loss and Unwanted Change at Forty

ANITA HIGMAN

I like order.

I placed my pretty new floral boxes in perfect rows on my closet shelf, each one housing neat stacks of organized photos and letters. Next to the boxes are dainty padded hangers with freshly cleaned clothes hanging without a wrinkle. All of the rows and stacks of perfectly ordered closet items had no idea that in sixty seconds the pipes would burst. Water would shower down in the bathroom and closets, destroying everything I had worked so hard to make just right.

I survived the mess.

Sometimes change doesn't hurt too much.

Sometimes change tries to kill us.

You won't see me raising my glass to that last one.

• • • • • •

DEAREST MODDY,

I am pathetic.

I don't know how you can stand my ongoing forty-year-old pity party. I can't even stand myself!!

Thank you for your endless patience with me. I am listening to your wise insights, even though it doesn't seem like I'm taking heed.

I know I still have lots of traveling to go on this road. My shoes are getting tattered from the sharp stones, and I can't say the view is worth much. It is my forty-footpath. The winding trail everyone must take, unless they die young.

When I was little, I didn't have to face too many unwanted changes. I was somehow kept from seeing too many horrors. Life wasn't really happy, but it was at least clear of too many monsters.

Now these unwanted trials called *change* make themselves at home in my life. I would order change to leave, but it would only sneak back in through a crack in the door.

Oh, Moddy, honestly, it's everywhere, like an airborne disease. I could shelter myself from it by taking up residency in an emotional fantasy world, but then I don't think that is such a positive alternative.

So. Here I am, Moddy.

I am in limbo waiting for change and loss and all the other scary goodies that come out of being that magical age of forty.

And even before I turned forty, I had already known loss.

I lost my own childhood. I never did find it. I lost all my grandparents in death and a number of my other relatives. I lost good friendships that just moseyed into the sunset and never returned. I have lost countless important career opportunities, and for no apparent reason.

I have lost babies in miscarriage. The first one happened in the hospital. No matter how heavily I bled, I just knew my baby would be OK. I just couldn't imagine this horror. That it could be happening to me. It was too much. But horror found me. My child had died inside of me. This very tiny and precious baby was a little girl. I named her Leah. I nearly cry as I write this because it is still hard.

And as you know, two years ago, I lost my mother. I loved her. Her death still hurts me. And as I wrote you recently, my friend's husband died, and the unexpected loss nearly scared me witless!

I have lost, and I hate it!!

All of this seems so pointless and such a waste for a God who is so frugal. I know loss and waste come from a broken world, but I believe life is just too hard sometimes. It is just too much for any living thing to deal with. Humanity is overwhelmed with grief. Perhaps Mars has a better deal going.

Once I wrote, "Even the hardest of winters . . . bequeaths us roses." I can write so wisely, Moddy. And all the pretty words are true, but I just think life's emotional winters are too long and too hard. Perhaps the winters are not worth the roses!! Could you please tell me what the point is? What is the good in all this loss?

And I know there will be more loss in the future. Perhaps the fantasy world is looking better all the time. What hope is there to escape this? None. So what can come from it? What are we left with? Help me, Moddy.

I look over these pages scribbled on my kitchen table and feel really goofy. I'm not even making sense. I'm just in one of those moments when I feel overwhelmed with this ugly, unwanted, unfair dimension of life. Why, Moddy? I don't understand God at all! In this moment, I have no clue as to why you do!

Love forever and always, from somebody caught throwing yet another earthly tantrum. I sense the angels shaking their heads at me. Are you, Moddy? This may be the first letter you just really don't want to answer! If so, I'll understand. I'll somehow get over it . . . but thanks for letting me know you'll care enough to at least read this scrambled mess. . . .

I think I'll go shopping! That should get me out of this funk! Just ignore this letter. I'll get over it. I always do! I love you,

—Anita

Losing Is the Price We Pay for Living

RUTH VAUGHN

It's Mother's Day and *I remember my mother.*

This year, sitting alone on the patio, I remember the time when she lost her physical health, including control of her body and her dignity. An active minister's wife, almost in an instant she was stricken with acute arthritis, to the degree that she could not move without assistance. I have told you before about how her body swelled to twice its normal size, and due to a misdiagnosis, all her teeth were pulled. To say the least, she was in pain!

That summer, the minister of the small village church where she was being treated asked my father to preach in a revival meeting. Mother declared her intention of attending each service. This was not shocking, for throughout her illness, she had never missed a service, arriving in a wheelchair and sitting in a huge chair prepared with pillows.

Her new absurd idea was that she planned to conduct a children's meeting before each revival service. Remember, she could not move without assistance. She was in a constant state of suffering. *The whole idea was impossible! But she did it!*

Each afternoon, with great difficulty, she was helped into the car, where we packed her in with pillows. At the church, in her specially prepared chair, we placed her in the most comfortable position possible. She responded in good humor, smiles, and laughter.

And then she gathered the children about her, taught them finger plays, action choruses, sang with them, prayed with them, and told them dramatic stories about God. Swollen, stiff, with no teeth, she expended every erg of energy and talent to *give what she could!*

I, the teenager observing, found her inscrutably amazing. *In the midst of tragic life change*, I found her *at peace*.

"Mother, why don't you hate all this?" I often demanded. This phrase is branded on my brain: "Child . . . Life is God's Earth School. I'm having a new learning. That's all!"

· · · · · ·

ANITA, MY LOVE,

I'm not shaking my head, nor do I want to ignore your letter. This is one of the most important letters you've written to me. I'm not wise enough to answer it adequately, but please let me try.

None of us wants to admit that change comes in spite of our best efforts! And with change come losses . . . *and* gains, although this may be difficult to believe just now.

I think Annie Dillard phrased it this way: "But as she has grown, her smile has widened with a touch of fear and her glance has taken on depth. Now she is aware of some of the losses you incur by being here—the extraordinary rent you have to pay as long as you stay."

As I've studied your letter, I observe your beginning to understand that from birth, life is a series of losses. You don't like it, but consider how essential for living *losses* are in each human life. It is true: We *leave* and *are left* and *let go* of much that we love. But with each necessary loss in life comes gain. Consider with me.

- You *left* your mother's arms to stand on your own two feet autonomously, thus you became a conscious, unique, and separate self . . . loss/gain.
- You *left* her hand for first grade, exchanging the illusion of absolute shelter and absolute safety for the triumphant anxieties of

being your own person among your peers and new learning challenges . . . loss/gain.
- You *left* home for college, and you became a moral, responsible adult self, discovering—within the limitations imposed by necessity—your freedoms and choices . . . loss/gain.
- You *left* your independent, autonomous life to marry Peter, and soon you gave up your impossible expectations to become a lovingly connected self, renouncing ideal visions of perfect friendship, marriage, children, and family life for the wonderful imperfections of all-too-human relationships . . . loss/gain.
- Your mother *left you* in death . . .

. . . and you know that soon, so soon, you will have to *let go* of Scott and Hillary to freely find their own life roads, and in confronting the many *losses* that are brought by death and time, you become a mourning and adapting self, finding change at every stage of life. And you will continue to find—until your last breath—opportunities for new challenging adventures, for new creative transformations, for new *gains replacing the losses.*

Anita, you have lived change for forty years. Now you face more change. As I have, two decades longer.

Let me briefly try to tell you what I've learned. Losing is the price we pay for living. Making our way from birth to death, we find our way through the pain of giving up and giving up and giving up some portion of what we hold dear. And each loss is linked to our gains!

Albert Camus wrote,

> Losing a loved one [or world], uncertainty about what we are, these are deprivations that give rise to our worst suffering. We may be idealistic, but we need what is tangible. It is by the presence of persons and things that we believe we recognize our certainty. And though we may not like it, at least we live with this necessity.

But the astonishing . . . thing is that these deprivations bring us the cure at the same time that they give rise to pain. Once we have accepted the fact of loss, we understand that the loved one [or world] obstructed a whole corner of the possible, pure now as a sky washed by rain. Freedom emerges from weariness. To be happy is to stop. Free, we seek anew, enriched by pain. And the perpetual impulse forward always falls back again to gather new strength. The fall is brutal, but we set out again.

When I had to leave an active beloved campus, move to another place, try to find a new way to live with Addison's disease, I studied Camus's quote and wrote in my journal,

I've been sitting here trying to think it through. He is right. He is right. It's just that it all hurts so much and requires so much courage to face . . . that I want to deny it. But he is right. What was not possible in the old world is possible now.

An important example is time for my sons. I am always here for them now. I can share everything with them now. And although I tried to be available when needed in the old world, I wasn't always. They didn't always come first. Now they can. And that is one way that when I "have accepted the fact of loss, [I] understand that the loved [world] obstructed a whole corner of the possible, pure now as a sky washed by rain. Freedom emerges. . . . Free, [I] seek anew, enriched by pain. . . ."

Yes, I think I understand what he is saying and I think he is right. I will build a new world, one I could never have known had the old one not been taken away. There will be, in that new world, relationships and adventures, possibilities and potentials, that were not available before. So although I did not wish that "corner of my world" to be "pure as sky washed by rain," it is! . . . and in that purity does lie opportunity for joyful things, happy experiences . . . a new world that could not have existed before.

That response to the Camus quote came from unexpected, unwanted change. I believe his words are equally relevant to the expected, wanted change, which is still a mighty painful *loss*. I've told you I lived most of my life as an only child with my much older parents. We were best friends. We were the Three Musketeers.

They knew, following high school, I would go on to college. It was an expected, wanted change but "brutal" because it meant the emptiness of their home. The "laughing sparkle" had gone away, never to return the same. Mother told me that as they walked into the staggering silence, she turned to my father. "No. You're not going to your office today. This is not an ordinary day; nor should we handle it as such. We are going on a picnic, a holiday. We are going to be two lovers alone again."

Don't you see? My presence "obstructed a whole corner of the possible, pure now as a sky washed by rain. Freedom emerges . . ." Mother was wise enough to challenge my father to move from the pain of the loss of their last child from their home to move directly into building a new relationship, exploring new possibilities, open to new adventures.

These are the expected, wanted changes. When I came to the empty house after enrolling my youngest son in kindergarten, I was deeply aware of *loss*. I wrote a poem:

To Ronnie's Kindergarten Teacher

To your expert hands, I now release
This blue-eyed child, I hold so dear . . .
Expected, wanted event . . .
but sober in perceiving *loss*. . . .

The last line:

I'll take care of his todays . . .
you, his tomorrows.

Of course, you remember when Hillary went to kindergarten, and you knew that both children, forevermore, were now in a world with other people guiding them to their own "tomorrows." More and more, they would move away from your constant motherly care and influence.

These are expected, wanted changes, but they do bring painful loss . . . *and gain.* . . . As the children begin to leave you, you are not bereft . . . for you can carefully create a new world, "pure now, as a sky washed by rain. Freedom emerges . . ." Loss/gain.

Anita, I would say one thing more of unexpected, unwanted change that erupts in the midst of expected normal living. It is this: We are moved by forces beyond our control (such as Addison's disease for me, your friend's husband's death in your recent life); we are also the active authors of our fate. *We make choices with God.* We are never victims. The poet said, "I am the captain of my soul!"

One way I have handled "blazing carousels" in the last two decades has been to whisper softly or sing *fortissimo* the words of an old hymn:

Fear not; I am with thee;
Oh, be not dismayed,
for I am thy God;
I will still give thee aid.
I'll strengthen thee, help thee,
and cause thee to stand,
Upheld by my gracious, omnipotent hand.

These words can change my entire emotional system when I sing:

When through fiery trials,
thy pathway shall lie,

My grace, all sufficient,
shall be thy supply.

But this couplet is the key for me:

For I will be with thee
thy trials to bless
and sanctify to thee
thy deepest distress.

When the lyric first came to my attention, I went to the dictionary to define "sanctify" and applied Webster's definition here:

to make holy . . . thy deepest distress;
to make sacred . . . thy deepest distress;
to make productive of spiritual blessing . . .
thy deepest distress.
In the words I use, to make *creative use of* . . .
my deepest distress.

Anita, this I believe: When we find loss, expected or unexpected, God will *sanctify* the loss, if we allow Him to. It is God's way to not waste anything. Jesus himself demonstrated on the cross that nothing need ever be wasted if He is on the scene.

Calvary happened to Jesus, but through it He experienced the Resurrection, the Ascension, a whole dispensation of grace—for us. From the darkness of one's personal Calvary, He surely can lead through Camelot-ashed-darkness to a plateau where I, you, every person, can create, with Him, a new world, a new carousel, a new happiness. *It is a choice.*

These are the bottom-line answers I would give to your scorching, painful questions exploring loss or unwanted change. You have to find your own answers, Anita, but these are the ones that satisfy me. I pray they will assist you to be "free, enriched by pain" to find

God's challenge of change . . . expected, unexpected . . . wanted, and unwanted.

I share with you one stanza and chorus of an old hymn that has brought me through heartbreaking losses more times than I can count:

Though the way seemed straight and narrow,
All I claimed was swept away;
My ambitions, plans, and wishes
At my feet in ashes lay.
I will praise Him!

In that stunning last-line determination, you can daily live Jesus' promise of the abundant life, no matter the circumstances of loss, disappointment, or pain. I promise!

Anita, we can discuss your letter more if you need to. The answer to the "funk" you were feeling is not to run away and put your mind on shopping. The answer is to "Be still, and know" God is with you in every moment of life, even in the painful changes. He is a Redeemer God; He will make creative use of each loss until, in each instance, you can find the gain! *I promise . . .*

. . . with all my love,

—Moddy

Exploring Service to Others at Forty

ANITA HIGMAN

All the lovely things I like to think I am and do get washed away in the daily grind of reality. Sometimes this is what I am left with:

I am a giver supreme!
Especially when you've offered first.
You bet I can help you.
That is, if the weather is warm enough.
Yes, I am most concerned about you.
What did you say your name was?
I believe in you all the way.
Unless, of course, you disappoint me.
You're a friend forever and always!
But forever is a difficult concept.
I always have time for you.
Did I mention my tight schedule?
Service to others sounds so majestic.
Too bad majestic is not "in" this year.

I wonder if Moddy has ever struggled with these little dark whispers.

• • • • • •

MY DEAR MODDY RUTH,

The lust to have it all.
What should I do about this grisly problem I have? It hasn't

reached epidemic proportions yet, but it is slowly growing in my emotional Petri dish. It is sneaking up my forty-footpath. Or should I say, it is slithering, if you know what I mean?

This problem tends to get worse at forty because I can see the end of life and what I have not yet accomplished. So what is acutely real to me today is the fact that these desires have become more intense instead of mellowing with age.

Commercials, books, movies, even some Christians hint at it. The whisper in my ear is, "Haven't you heard? You can have it all! The brass ring. A successful career . . . plenty of cash . . . children . . . an impressive house . . . be well-known and well-liked . . . good health. . . . And all of this can be wrapped up in a pretty Christian package destined for heaven." After all, "Ask and you shall receive." Right?

But sometimes I have wondered, *What sacrifices must be made to have it all? Will my achievement come at the expense of the needs of others? Will I have to say a lot of no's to people to reach my long-term goals?* Perhaps some of the no's should be yeses. Oh, Moddy, how do I know? Perhaps someone really needs my financial assistance, or my encouragement, my time, my listening ear. Perhaps I have been called to a higher purpose than spending all my time and energy to make *my* dreams come true. I wrestle with this dilemma often.

I looked in my book of famous quotes under "ambition," and almost all of them were very negative. None of them made ambition look like something pretty to take home to Momma.

My point is that my many ambitions and my own personal desires may be keeping me from giving to others the way I should.

Years ago some friends were moving. At such times I am never at my peak performance when it comes to friendship. I can always think of a million things I desperately have to do careerwise (or anywaywise) when a friend needs help moving. Or when someone needs me to baby-sit. Or when the church needs a day of yard work done. I tend to fade away, and then conveniently reappear when friends are ready again just to have lunch or go to a movie or when the church is ready to have a fun banquet.

So that you don't think I am a total lost cause, I have helped friends in their times of need, I have been a part of the church food pantry, I have taught Sunday school, I have baby-sat, and I have done volunteer work at various times in my life.

But these marvelous moments of service to others are tainted. There is this ever-so-slight feeling that I was doing it out of obligation to God rather than out of love for Him and His creation. Now, I know if I wait until all my motivations are perfect in every way, I will never get to do any good deeds for anyone! Herein lies the rub, as Shakespeare would say.

The popular notion is for everyone to concentrate on "Number One." I know in my heart that isn't the right way to live, and yet . . . "Number One" always seems so deserving of our immediate attention!

I remember times when I did reach out to people who I thought were in emotional or financial need. They ended up using me and taking advantage of my generosity.

Years ago I did volunteer work in a nursing home. The residents didn't seem to appreciate it very much, and a number of the workers seemed even to resent my being there. Eventually I just gave it up. I guess I couldn't handle not being appreciated.

Through many of these situations, I have discovered something about myself. I do not like serving other people with a whole heart and then being squashed like a bug. I can't seem to pop myself back out like the little animals in the cartoons when they are *ka-blammered* on the head. I am a Christian, but I am still a human being. I can do this giving thing for a while, but then I usually peter out under the weight of trying to be what I am not fully committed to in my heart.

In the end, I suppose I am more committed to what I am having for lunch than what the woman living under the bridge downtown is having for lunch. But then, could I really serve her lunch every day? How could I pull that off for the long haul? Would she even want me to? Sometimes service is unwelcome and complicated and confusing and even disheartening. Sometimes it doesn't make me feel cozy inside.

So look where I am left, Moddy. Stuck in an imperfect world, doing imperfect things for imperfect people!

What do we do? How are we to be? Help me to know how you became so generous in this way. You are such a fine person to ask this question of because I know you don't just give to people—you serve them with your whole heart. And it's a joy to know you, remembering my visions of you in my youth and now in this adult period when we've taken off our masks to share through letters. You give me hope, Moddy, because I honestly desire to have a better heart in this way. After all, how could I do less for Him who came to earth as a servant?

Please don't despair, but I'm afraid the truth is that you're receiving love in this letter from someone who still has trouble sharing her dolly!

—Anita

We Can Act or We Can React

RUTH VAUGHN

Today our minister began his sermon with this anecdote from the life of Gandhi, the holy man of India . . . a Hindu, of course. A young, enthusiastic American missionary had gone to India to present the gospel of Jesus.

Knowing this was Gandhi's land, he decided to take the courage to try to make an appointment with Gandhi for a few minutes alone. Because of the young man's persistence, the interview was granted. He explained his mission, concluding, "I would be grateful to know your advice to me as I try to be a Protestant missionary."

Gandhi studied the excited, exuberant youth before him and said, "Young man, your best contribution to the people of India is *to be like Jesus.*"

The little story moved me deeply. Gandhi did not believe Jesus was the Son of God, but he had studied His life, His words, His actions enough to know that, regardless of theology, the best gift anyone could give anywhere, anytime, anyway, is "to be like Jesus." And I whispered my deepest yearning:

"Help me, every day, in every way, to *be like Jesus!*"

• • • • • •

ANITA, MY LOVE,

How I rejoice in your honesty, your realism, your heart-purity! Thank you for being you!

Yes, it would be wonderful if each of us could have it all, going full steam ahead toward our personal dreams as well as helping other people fulfill their dreams! But as you say so eloquently, this is not life! So what to do? That, my dear, is the question!

Let me begin with this: There are two kinds of people in the world.

First, there are those who are wrapped up in themselves with no time, no interest, no concern for others.

Second, there are those who take time, interest, energy to be interested in others.

The first may be called the *Here I am!* kind of person. The latter may be called the *There you are!* kind of person.

We were all born to shout *"Here I am!"* hoping everyone around us will bask in the wonders of our own *selves*! I remember clearly my first insight into this. I may have been only five. My father took me to visit the poorest family I had ever seen. They had ten children, all dressed in tatters, huddling around a potbellied wood-burning stove in a house where rags were stuffed around the windows to keep out the wind.

As the children and I moved into a room where we could be separate from the adults, I honestly had the feeling that they would be thrilled, maybe even honored, to hear me tell about my life. They listened to my dramatic recital in stoic silence, unimpressed, uninterested. I vividly remember my bewilderment: These poor children were not remotely responding to my account of my exciting life!

In the strained silence of that shivering-cold room, it dawned on me that each of these children were as valuable as myself, their lives were as wonderful, to them, as my own. I simply didn't have the perception to *know, or to care to know!*

I was so ashamed, I could feel my face burn. And then, huddling in that cold room with these children whose lives were so alien to my own, I realized the choice I could make. I could be taken up with only myself and bore them all—and go away with no thought of returning—*or* I could focus on each of these children, learn their names, their ages, their interests, their dreams . . . that we might become *friends*!

It was at that time that I think I knew there were two kinds of people in the world—which I now interpret as *Here I am!* people and *There you are!* people. What kind of person did I want to be?

I knew the answer. Oh yes. With a full heart, I tried to get to know those children, to like them, to hope they would like me. The older girl, holding the infant, told me she had only seen one movie in her life, but she knew she wanted to be an actress! (Remember, Anita, I am very old! This was before television, and in my father's church, no one went to the movies because that was considered *sinful*!) But as Dottie told me breathlessly of the one movie she had seen, my own drama instincts thrilled with her desires.

She then gave the baby to another child and she role-played the movie for me, pulling in her siblings to help in the drama they had obviously enacted many times. I applauded enthusiastically. We agreed we would spend more time together, creating new plays in which we could both star! When I left that home, I had a group of friends. There was only one reason for it: I had chosen to focus on *There you are!*

Dottie and I became fast friends, and, indeed, we became actresses in small plays my mother wrote for us to perform in *Juniors*, the hour prior to the Sunday evening service. Via the mail, we are still friends, even to this day.

The insight was important at the tender age of about five, but I knew its truth had to be developed consciously every day of my life from that moment on, if it were to be effective. And it is so *difficult*! Our own lives are so enchanting, Anita, it is an act of disciplined *choice* to focus on the lives of others who may be boring, or even completely disagreeable.

Which brings me to the second thing I would mention in this letter. I have learned that we can either be *actors* in response to others or *reactors*. I discovered this from a girl who had been hired to write letters for a rich elderly lady in our parish. I went with my friend one afternoon to the rich lady's house. The woman was rude, sarcastic, unpleasant the entire hour. When the letters were finished and ready for mailing, my friend stood and said, "Thank you for being so good to me in this job. I'll mail your letters and look forward to seeing you next week." And then, Anita . . . and then . . . she leaned down and kissed the woman's wrinkled cheek!

As soon as we were outside, I confronted her. "Why were you so nice to her when she was so dreadful to you?" Jenny grinned. "She can tell me the content of the letters to write, but she can*not* tell me how to *act*!" I have never forgotten her wisdom.

That long-ago day I understood that a person can respond to me unpleasantly and I can react in the same manner. Or I can *choose* to focus on the person, try to understand the reason for his or her anger, bitterness, or whatever unknown makes the person so unpleasant, and then deliberately *act as I choose*. It is a most difficult lesson, but vital if I am to be of service to others.

Recently, at a dinner party in my home, a close personal friend became so angry at something I had said that he actually ran from the table screaming and hid in the bathroom. We all gaped in astonishment. I had never dreamed my conversation with him would cause a negative response, much less volatile outrage. His wife and I smiled our mutual pain. Honestly wondering what to do, I looked directly across the table at a gracious-looking gentleman and asked a question, to which he quickly responded with long details. In our agony, we loved this man dearly! He was saving the party. We continued to ask questions to keep him going. And he obliged. On and on and on.

It seemed it would be forever. We all felt we must be near death in our embarrassment, wondering whatever to do with the man in the bathroom. I, as a woman, could not go to him; neither his wife nor any man, including Bob, seemed so inclined, and so we continued our frozen, smiling conversation until he, at long last, quietly returned. I got up, put my arms around him, and asked him to forgive me for my words. He gave a loud defense of the intention of his own words, and when he finished, I again asked if he would forgive me for my misunderstanding, asking if we could forget it and have a pleasant evening.

"You're the one still talking about it!" he roared.

I turned to the same gracious person with another question; again, he obliged by giving another fully detailed response . . . so lengthy that by the time his second monologue was concluded, the atmosphere was sparkling with laughter, camaraderie, and love. It is a happy memory . . . and it is a true story.

But, of course, I give this example from the age of sixty. It has not *always* been my response. I am still trying to learn this difficult lesson. It has been fifty-five years since my childhood effort to focus on others, and a few years later when I learned from my teenage friend to try to practice this truth: *In spite of the actions of others, we do not have to react. We can choose our own actions!*

It can be so easy to say the three words, "Please forgive me." And yet they can be the hardest words to articulate! They stick in our throats, especially when we feel we did nothing wrong. But even when we know we have done something needing forgiveness, the words can be hard to say. Yet I promise you, Anita, that these three words, whether deserved or undeserved, defuse hot spots more quickly, more thoroughly, than any other formula I know.

Consider this: Be the first to forgive, the first to say the words, whenever there is strain in any way where these words can calm. If practiced often enough, they become easier to say. If never practiced, they may become *impossible* to say!

So . . . although you may know and try to practice these important truths in best serving others, there remain the elements of *time and energy!* With families and careers, what does God expect of us in giving service to others in blocks of time and ergs of energy?

My best answer is rooted in this poem by Annie Johnson Flint. Since my youth, Anita, I have honestly spent large blocks of time studying, pondering, praying in its challenge. Let me share it with you.

Christ has no hands but our hands
To do His work today;
He has no feet but our feet
To lead men in His way.
He has no tongue but our tongues
To tell men how He died;
He has no help but our help
To bring them to His side.
We are the only Bible
The careless world will read;
We are the sinner's Gospel;
We are the scoffer's creed;
We are the Lord's last message
Written in deed and word—
What if the line is crooked?
What if the type is blurred?
What if our hands are busy
With other work than His?
What if our feet are walking
Where sin's allurement is?
What if our tongues are speaking
Of things His lips would spurn?
How can we hope to help Him
Unless from Him we learn?

Isn't this true? Do people find Jesus in our lives? That is the vital question. But the poet challenges us: Does the scoffer use our life to illustrate what being a Christian is *not*? I find that frightening.

What about active church involvement? What about community involvement? What about world involvement? In my personal hierarchy of values, I have always known I had to spend blocks of time and energy outside my family and career to answer the challenge of this poem. It is part of who I have chosen to become. It may be that, in future decades, God will direct my life to spend even more time and energy outside of home and career.

Writing books, Anita, is a form of ministry to God. I find it vital. But it is for the masses, chiefly unknown to me. I believe that God requires me to try to follow in His steps, to be as nearly like Jesus as possible. I have just reread this poem for the thousandth time, and my whole being surges in yearning to be available for those in my immediate world who need a representative of God with loving arms, listening ears, a caring heart . . . a real live human! "God with skin on," as it were. I can never do it perfectly, but oh, I do want to *try*! Should that not be the first priority of each Christian's life? The answer I have chosen is *yes*.

I have professional friends whose answer is *no*. Mass ministry consumes all their time and energy. I respect that completely. I can only say it is not true for *me*! If someone reads a book and writes a response, pleading for personal help . . . in my schedule, that has to be *priority*. If a family member or friend calls or comes to my home in need of counsel, or even for camaraderie, I try to stop everything.

Anita, this is a terribly personal choice. It comes from a personal relationship that is unique between each individual and his or her God. I believe my professional friends are correct in their own assessments; I value their conclusions as God's guidance for their lives. I believe each of us must respond in the uniqueness of *self with God*.

You may find your answers, your philosophy, the same as these professional friends of mine. If so, I applaud you. Honestly. Completely—with enthusiasm for your ministry.

If you do feel a divine command to personal ministry outside of career and family, there are innumerable ways to minister: Sunday school teaching, hot-line phone counseling, even becoming a *clown*!

That last one shocks me in the same dimension it delighted me when I first read of Betty Cozzens, who went to Clown School at age sixty-five. Since that time, with arthritis and a bad leg, her calendar began to fill with benefit dates for groups like the Cystic Fibrosis Foundation, and gigs at hospitals for sick or handicapped kids. She looks like all professional clowns: big red nose, orange scare wig, whiteface makeup, patchwork suit, doing all the crazy things clowns do. "Sometimes I get tired," she admits. "So then I take out a puppet and perform sitting down. You do get tired, but it's a different kind of tired, a satisfied kind of tired."

My brother Lyman is a chaplain for the college church in Bethany, Oklahoma. He and his wife, both age seventy-six, are given weekly assignments to visit those who are frail, ill, or lonely in the huge congregation. One late evening recently, they stopped by our home after a dinner party. They used the same words as Betty Cozzens in her clown ministry, although they were dressed in ministerial formality: "You do get tired, but it's a different kind of tired, a satisfied kind of tired."

There are so many ways to be of service to others, no matter your age. Some women in our church, in all age groups, bake cookies every Monday, to be served the following Sunday to first-time visitors. I would love that, but I think I'd love being a clown more!

I was in a clown troupe when I was a college freshman, performing monthly for local children's hospitals. But my schedule quickly outgrew it. I had not thought of it again until I read this article. Could there come a time in my life when God would find my best ministry away from the computer . . . in a clown suit, bringing Jesus to kids needing His laughter, His presence, His love? If so, I would enjoy it with the same gusto I enjoy my present life.

You observed me on a college campus. I spent many hours teaching classes, but you also know that I spent many hundreds of hours in personal counseling. I knew the academics were important for the future of my students. But my authentic loving concern for them was perhaps more vital. In the first session of each class, I would give my home phone number, saying, "I am available anytime of the day or night if you need me for any reason." My students took full advantage of this! They not only came to my home at 2:00 A.M., but I frequently went to them in the dorm at 2:00 A.M., when things seemed to become the most greenery-yallery-hopeless. The SNU president, Dr. Cantrell, tells of the many times he would be going to his office at 7:00 A.M. to find me running from one of the girls' dorms to make my 7:30 class. "I always prayed for you," he says, "but worried about your health!"

In the years when I was housebound with the seemingly insoluble complications of Addison's disease, I wrote stage plays to which the mail response was enormous. It was a phenomenon. My only explanation for it is that the fragility of my health was well known. The lines written in the plays reflected my knowledge of human loss, human suffering, human bewilderment. Somehow these dramas developed rapport between the audience and the unseen playwright. They knew I understood much of the human condition.

As I consider the incredible response by correspondence, I believe it came because these people felt they could share with me their innermost secrets, without having to look into my brown eyes and whisper them. I believe it was in their anonymity that hundreds of men and women dared to trust me, dared to reach out to me with their scrawled sharings, and I responded.

In those seven years, I'm sure I wrote thousands of personal letters. In that faithfulness, all unseen, I could go through life traumas with people personally unknown to me, who became some of my dearest friends. This is true today. I am still in contact with dozens of people whom I have never once seen in person. Of course, many met me through reading the books I've been writing since the age of twenty-two . . . and *many* by attending my plays and musicals those seven years when, with a frighteningly fragile body, I was resident playwright of a huge drama program.

On my computer desk today, I have a framed note from a woman unknown to me who wrote, "We who watched your plays will never forget you. Your spirit walks softly among us still. I carry your letters in my Bible. I share them often with others who are hurting." When I received that note a few years ago, I could only gasp in astonishment. I honestly have no memory of corresponding with a person by that name, but it is obvious that I did write her faithfully during a "hurting time" in her life.

I have just reread your letter in which you are pondering God's directives for your life in being of service to others in our world of computers, technology, and distance. In this era, it seems relationships have changed. Heart-sharing closeness is harder to find. One man who frequently writes from Detroit tells me he has many acquaintances at work but he knows none of them personally. He is not involved in church or community. "The world is so impersonal," he tells me. Sad as it is, I—a woman he has never met except in book pages—am his "best friend, his most trusted confidante." In my priorities, I feel I must be faithful to him to be worthy of his faith in the woman who wrote books that made him feel my hand holding his.

This world can be very impersonal for people even in "America's

Heartland," even in Oklahoma and Texas. Study, ponder, and pray over Annie Johnson Flint's beautiful poetic challenge, and seek to be a *There you are!* kind of person.

Let's be *the Lord's last message written in deed and word.* And see the tragedy *if the line is crooked . . . if the type is blurred!*

And let's hold hands across space in prayer that God will guide us to live in such a way that we can be "the only Bible the careless world will read." We can never do it perfectly. My life is so heavy with personal and professional obligations, it's hard to break the barriers to personally care for others, whether in person, by phone, or by letter. No, we can't do it perfectly, but let's *try!*

I pray with you . . . please pray with me.

—Moddy

chapter fourteen

Doing Life at Forty

ANITA HIGMAN

Every morning I try to relax with a cup of coffee in our garden room. This spot in our home is a bright yet cozy glassed-in room that overlooks our backyard. With the children upstairs doing their wild getting-ready-for-school things, I look forward to these quiet early-morning moments with God.

BUT . . . someday when my kids are all grown up and gone, these quiet moments will be everywhere in the house . . . *all day . . . every day.*

I wonder if I will cherish the quiet as much then. Perhaps it will become an enemy as well as a friend.

I am scared out of my wits when I think about it too long.

But somewhere deep inside there's the tiniest spark of thought that maybe *God has a plan for those years too* . . . and that it really will be OK.

I wonder what Moddy did with her empty nest.

· · · · · ·

DEAR MODDY,

I know this may sound crazy, but I've come up with a phrase I like. Let me try it on for you. Moddy, with every fiber of my being I want to "do life"!

What do you think of that phrase? I like the words, but let me try to explore what I think they may mean to me. I wonder what they'll mean to you.

Here I am forty years old, and sometimes I still wonder if I'm even beginning to do what I should be doing with my life. Should I have gotten my Master's degree? Should I have studied harder? Should I have traveled more? My spirit can tangle with so many "should haves."

But you've challenged me this year that the more important question is, "Can I do it now?"

In a few years my children will be grown. I wonder if I should be preparing for that in some way, so that I have a life plan for the time when our nest is empty.

I have already experienced the first level of the empty nest, in that my kids are both in school. But waving good-bye to them for college and independence and marriage and beyond is a horse of a different color. And it looks like a dark, brooding mare to me!

It means not seeing my kids every day to talk about what is thrilling them or hurting them. No more straightening her hair bows and playing his favorite card game with him. Not feeling that 3:30 rush anymore when they whirl in from school full of delicious talk about their day. This is going to be much harder to swallow. Like trying to eat a whole watermelon in one gulp.

Not a pretty sight.

So, maybe I need to be thinking and praying about all this transition. It could get hairy, not to mention how Peter and I might perceive each other. One day, suddenly, we will be just husband and wife again. That will be another massive adjustment, because we have felt more like Mom and Dad than sweethearts for a long time now.

On another forty angle, someone told a friend something like this: "Don't you think it's about time you changed your hairstyle? I mean, you're older now. Women of your age aren't supposed to have long hair." As I recall, the friend was only in her thirties.

Remembering that story makes me think how society puts limitations on certain decades of our lives. It is easy to get sucked into that mentality. But another part of me wants to rejoice and scream, "I want to fly. If it means with long hair at fifty, what does it really matter?"

Yes, Moddy, Anita at forty is still wanting to fly and dream. As much if not more than when you watched me fly and dream on a college campus. Once I wrote, "A carriage filled with dreams goes nowhere without the courage to draw it." Don't you like that? I want the courage to draw my God-given dreams into the next forty years or more.

You've helped me understand clearly that, at forty, there are so many things yet to do! Things for which I have been told I am gifted. Things that would bring such joy to others, and to my own family. For instance, I want to raise a small garden of tomatoes. I want to volunteer at a soup kitchen. I want to learn to speak Spanish. I want to take my kids to the park more often. I want to read and write more. I want to see the Holy Land. I want to learn to prepare French cuisine. I want to serve it for the church teen formal banquet. I want to love more.

I've just reread your letter about Annie Johnson Flint's challenge. Oh yes, Moddy, like you, I do want to be all of these things. I know I can never do it perfectly, either, but I can sure give it a shot!

There's another thing, Moddy, that I would talk to you about. I know I don't want to do these things just to be busy. I want to be and do what I am and what I am meant to be in the future. I don't want immature motivations honking their horns at me and demanding that I come for a ride. I'm really trying to "discover the *why* and the *who*" of the real identity of Anita Higman—to bubble forth and celebrate life. Not a figment of what society desires, but what the Creator saw the day he wove me together in my mother's womb.

What do you think, Moddy dear? Should I fly? Or should I cut my hair, so to speak?

Is what I am doing right now on schedule, preparing me for what I should do the rest of my life? Should I think about changes in myself, in my philosophy? The discussions in our letters this year have changed me a lot, including the challenge to be an *actor* and not a *reactor*, to focus on others, to study and ponder Annie Johnson Flint's words. It's like every event of this significant year has somehow been specially designed to help me learn more clearly the lessons I've been searching for.

But I'm not there yet, as you well know. But you tell me you're not there yet either . . . so it's good to know that I am forty and you are sixty . . . and we are still growing up . . . but isn't it fun that we can do it together?

I love you, Moddy,

—Your college kid
still needing your love,
Anita

It's Never Too Late to Be What You Might Have Been

RUTH VAUGHN

DEAR ANITA,

I found this in an ancient scrapbook today:

> In 1955 leading citizens of a large city inserted prophecies of life twenty years future in a time capsule, which was placed in a new building. One of these predictions read: "In 1975 men and women will still struggle for happiness—which will continue to lie within themselves."

1955, 1975 . . . I laughed aloud at the ancient dates that had seemed so current when I clipped the article and put it in a scrapbook. I am glad I kept it. For their prediction will be as true, of course, in the twenty-first century as it has been in the twentieth.

Perhaps the city fathers in 1955 were striving to clarify the words of the Declaration of Independence—that we have an inalienable right to the "pursuit of happiness." This gives me the thought that joy must be sought to be found. But those who have joined the search have found joy to be like a shadow . . . following close by when unheeded, but dashing away when chased. For *happiness comes from within!*

When I was in graduate school, one of my colleagues was clocked driving at 115 miles per hour before surrendering to the police. When asked why he was racing, he grinned. "I was chasing a thrill!" It was the truth of his life, I knew.

One night at a multifamily picnic, he moved away from the group to *go inward in thought*. He watched the soaring fire that swayed and danced. He beheld the faces of the children playing games on the sand. When their mothers stopped the play and pointed upward toward the gold-studded sky, their faces held wonder like a cup. Suddenly, aloof from the crowd, he knew the hot sting of tears. He *felt the presence of God.* He bowed his head reverently and wept in worship for the first time in his adult life. Later, he told me, "God had only been theory to me, until that night when I relaxed and exposed my heart to the beauty of His creation. And then . . . all unannounced! . . . all unsought! . . . *God came to me!*"

The city fathers were wise half a decade ago: *Happiness lies within.*

Anita, I like it! your phrase, *doing life!*

For years, I've been a fan of the television series *Kung Fu.* I still see it occasionally on reruns. The young protagonist's name is Peter. To identify himself separately from his father, the Chinese holy man Caine, Peter proclaims loudly at every show's beginning, "I'm a cop! That's who I am! That's what I do!"

I love this fictional Peter and I identify with him. I spend much time in the world of mechanical geniuses like my husband. I barely know a bolt from a screw, have never dealt with either of them overtly, and anything with motors or electronic innards leaves me baffled. To all the teasing about my ignorance, I often respond as dramatically assertive as Peter: "I'm a writer. That's who I am. That's what I do!"

Well, of course, what we do is not the *who* of Peter, of Ruth, or any person. For that reason, in some circles, it is the law of good breeding to never ask, "What do you *do?*" This is, perhaps, especially sensitive for women who reply, "I'm just a wife, a mother." Too often, the answer begs defense, as if this is not the most important, most demanding, most vital profession possible.

I know. When I was in the academic world of Kansas University, it was obvious I was in graduate school. But still there came the inevitable question, "What do you *do?*" With full dignity, I would respond, "I write books, plays, a newspaper column . . ." Not once did I *ever* tell these high-minded people that I also drove a sixty-six-passenger school bus twice a day, taking three groups of children to and from home. Although I glowed about my homelife, they considered me *more* than a homemaker. Only a few ever cared to know the most important element of introduction: Who is Ruth, the person? In that world, we were wrapped up in our *doing, in our achieving . . . what we did was who we were!* Only a few of us got to know real people.

In these letters, we have discussed the vital truth of personal identity. We have to *be* in order to *do anything effectively*. Do you know the proverb "A man must do. A woman need only be"? The inference is that *to be* is passive. *To be* is to sit there, empty. In that sense, to be is *not* to be. But this is not always true.

When Mary sat quietly at Jesus' feet until Martha shouted her frustration of her much *doing* without Mary's help, He said quietly, "Mary has chosen the better part." Both women were doing, but in different ways. There is no being without doing; thinking is an act, so is sitting at Jesus' feet listening, or, in our time, praying. Jesus' response to Martha is the truth that *to do* is not to keep a house or build a career or make money; *to do* is to bring meaning to time.

We have talked about the relentless pace of time and the *choices* we have to make to give the greatest purpose to our earthly life. Anita, some of us (like you and me) are able to make our living in an occupation we would do for *free* because we love what we do so much! Some make a living doing things they consider relatively meaningless, but can choose to give their own time for other kinds of doing: doing things for art, for fun, for helping the ill, the elderly, the homeless, the children, and for the growth of their minds or the good of the human race.

One of my friends works on the assembly line of Ford Motor Company. He has spent forty hours a week in the same job for twenty-one years. His love is the cello, which he practices daily, teaches private lessons, performs in the church orchestra. This is his chief *doing*, his best identity line.

One of my students now owns his own construction company. We were chatting recently of his deep involvement in fathering his three children. Speaking of all the time required in the summer, especially, he laughed. "When people ask what I do, I tell them I administrate a construction company on the side, but my career is coaching Little League!"

This is why I like your term: *doing life*! "Your life begins at forty" is the old cliché, and as most clichés, it is breathtakingly true! Browning said it: "The last of life, for which the first was made."

Through history, age forty has been a strategic time in which one can only get better and better . . . or go into a funk. Sarah Vaughan has just kept caroling the world and, at sixty-three, said, "My voice just gets better and better." On the other hand, Beethoven slid into a five-year halt at forty! Finally, he pulled himself up and went on to compose his seventh, eighth, and ninth symphonies and all his late quartets (from Opus 130 on). Forty can often be a crossroads. You can go into a funk or you can "get better and better!"

Let's consider another challenge you're facing at forty: *Is this what I want to do for the rest of my life?* You wrote a top-of-the-head list, but how about spending time to work on one idea seriously? I love the George Eliot line "It's never too late to be what you might have been."

Consider. As your children grow away from you, would it be challenging to explore additional degrees in order to teach your writing craft in college? You probably could teach high school now with perhaps only additional hours of certification rather than another degree. Anyway, I thought I would mention this: I read recently that in the nation's colleges this year, more than one in ten students is *over fifty*.

I challenged all my female collegians: "Include the education block in your degree program. You may never use it, but it is good to have." Have you thought of how you would support the family if, for any reason, Peter's income was lost? I know you could work somewhere to have a solid salary for your writing . . . but do consider: Teaching is a degree that opens the door to a world where you would have the same daily schedule, the same holidays, and free summers as your children do.

Of course, this is the one thing that, from my background, I obviously would suggest. I loved teaching creative writing on a university campus. I recommend it highly!

Anita, you were there. You know how I *joyed* the years on a university campus as a professor. But I can tell you that I'm grateful I moved on from the campus to do other things, climb other mountains, learn other things. I look now at my colleagues, nearing retirement after a lifetime of teaching, and I rejoice in the fulfillment for their lives. But in my own life, I would tell you that I am thrilled *I did that, have the T-shirt!* . . . but that my life adventure moved on into other interests and challenges.

I was a published author when I entered graduate programs, but it became a heart-passion to be able to teach to others what I loved! Later I wrote a book compressing the essence of that degree program. It is titled *Write to Discover Yourself.* Its readers still tell me how it challenged, educated, and in some cases literally formed the direction of their future. As a published author, you might want to think of a graduate program. Anytime a woman comes from her "empty nest" sighing, "The kids have their lives; my husband has his life; I have nothing to do" . . . my first quick response is: "Go back to school!" This, of course, is my personal bias!

Yesterday was the monthly luncheon of Oklahoma Women Pilots. Because of Bob's passion for the years he flew his own planes, I am a well-established part of the "Lunch Bunch"! The "girl" who sat across the table from me is an attorney.

I said to her, "I've never had time to ask, but I'm so eager to know: Why did you choose to be an attorney?" She told me the story and the fulfillment she had found for seventeen years.

I enthused, "Had such a career been a possibility for me when I was eighteen, I do believe that is what I would have chosen!" Quickly, she said, "Well, do it now!" At my startled look, she demanded, "How old are you?" When I told her sixty, she said, "Enroll this fall. Three years will fly by, and at the age of sixty-three, you'll be a lawyer! Do it!" Gulping, I explained I had a fulfilling career and there was no time for another. There just isn't time for it all! Never will be!

I do think I could have been as great in criminal law defense as the silver-tongued Johnnie Cochran in the famous O. J. Simpson trial. But when I was eighteen, to my knowledge, no woman ever remotely considered becoming a lawyer. Oh, I'd love it now! I know I would, but there just is not going to be *time*. Even if I'm still active at 109!!

But, Anita, at this recent Lunch Bunch, I thought of you. In this era with so many years of vigorous life still possible for all of us, if I wanted to change professions, I still could become a lawyer . . . I could still pilot my own plane . . . if I thought that was good stewardship of my time! I don't. I'm twenty years older than you are. I have to cherish time more carefully! Precious time!!

So . . . let me give your own question back to you. Who do you want to be when you grow up? Of course, you have an answer at the age of forty, but yes, I would urge you to ask it again! You wrote a quickie list. Think of writing an earnest one.

Events of life may choose for you, but if nothing unexpected happens, your future can indeed be a personal choice. So dream away as if you were eighteen again! Wanna be a university professor . . . or a skilled lawyer . . . or a pilot? Or do you want to write books, newspaper columns, work in a soup kitchen and create French cuisine for formal affairs? If God guided me, I could do them all, including French cuisine! I used to be quite a gourmet chef. Bet you didn't know that about me, did you?

But at forty, Anita, be open to God's guidance for your future. Do you want to win the Pulitzer Prize, put one of your plays on Broadway, be the next Erma Bombeck . . . or . . . when the children are in college, do you feel God might guide you to be a persuasive pleader for the oppressed in *three years!* . . . or you could choose to wing air lanes in all the glory to which my women pilot friends constantly refer.

Forty is a new beginning!

I promise: In the next decades, you can make choices that are more fulfilling, more satisfying in your professional and personal life than you have dreamed until this half-time crisis when you are stopping long enough to carefully consider how you want to *do life* in your future . . . as it looms now . . . aware of unexpecteds that could interrupt your best-laid plans!

I suggest, really: Go back to list-making. Column it with your future decades headlined on top: 40 . . . 50 . . . 60 . . . 70 . . . 80 . . . 90.

Then ponder: What do you want to do *most* in this decade? I believe your answer would be "mother Scott and Hillary" with everything else secondary. But at fifty, what would be your list with both children autonomous adults? As my mother told my father when I went to college, "We are two lovers facing life alone again," so will you two be. What will be your priorities then? What will you and Peter do in the best stewardship of energies, interests, and *time* at fifty?

Can I include here my personal opinion of how to best parent young adults? It is one word: *Don't.* To my adult sons with their own families, their own careers, their own lives, I try to be their best cheerleader. We heart-share on occasion, but I try never to give a word of advice unless asked. This frees them to grab their gold trophies of success or fall facedown in their own failures. It frees me from the responsibility of trying to make their lives perfectly happy. When they were small, I could kiss them, give them an ice cream cone, and make things "all better!" That is no longer in my power. And I have enough sense to know it! "Run free . . . of me" is my challenge to adult children, knowing that inherent in the gift of freedom is the other side of the same coin: *unconditional forever love.* They have a safety net in our love . . . they can never be lost . . . and they know it!

Back to the letter! Column 50. Anita, consider life as you would like to *do it* in that decade. I can tell you that in our fifties, Bob and I both expanded the uniquely diverse careers we loved but were more daring in exploration.

It was after my balloon-decorated fiftieth birthday party that I chose to travel through the U.S. and Canada, speaking in seminars and retreats and teaching creative writing workshops, even on a cruise ship! It was a new dimension of endeavor for me, and as I have mentioned, I did not publish a book in the eleven years following age forty-eight. My thirty-ninth book was published at age fifty-nine.

The travel-speaking schedule was exciting, exhilarating, expanding all my horizons, with adults of both sexes and all ages coming to listen to my words. Like my experience on a college campus, I am grateful for it, but I would never want to do it again!

Perhaps it was in my fifties that I finally came to terms with my limitations. I had always assumed that anything I wanted badly enough, I could achieve. In fifty years I had proved those powers in many ways. But one ordinary day when I was prowling the university library, for the first time *impossibility* hit me like a loaded freight train. Honestly, Anita, I felt like wailing at the insight that never, ever, in my lifetime would I have the possibility of reading all the books

I had planned to read before my death. It was like an *epiphany* for me, an awakening to new knowledge about life.

The fact that one cannot read all the books in a lifetime is such a *given*, it amazes me that it pained me so deeply. But I threw myself into a chair in a nearby carrel, grabbed a spiral notebook, and scrawled, "My assumption that I could accept any challenge if I set my mind to it has been rooted, not in arrogance, but in sheer naïveté. I have understood I would never know Einstein's formulas, nor the engine formula for Bob's backyard pond-pump, but I didn't want to know. I did want to know all the works of Tolstoy, Jane Austen, Hemingway, C. S. Lewis, *and Annie Dillard!* There is no time to read all of them, much less consider experiencing all the authors, old and new, whose books I have never opened. I have my breath back from the pain of accepting the many things I will never learn. *It's the finality that hurts!*"

That is my honest journal record! But, Anita, in a way, that pain was silly, don't you think? I believe there is heaven . . . don't they have the *best* library there? Who knows? But the knowledge of God's heaven soothes the pain of knowing that, on this earth, there are many joys we will never know, for there is not that much *time!* In the "larger life," we'll have plenty of *time!* Ah! The luxury!

Let's move on to Column 60: Ponder what things you would put on that decade list. What would you like to be when you grow to be this awesome age?

I'll tell you one thing: Your body will have changed since forty. But that isn't all bad. There are compensations. In this sixth decade, Bob and I find ourselves seriously considering what we deem might be the best stewardship of energies, interests, and *time* still available to us. There can easily be three more decades of vital, vibrant *doing life* . . . but we have confronted the time theory: *Use it or lose it!* We spend dinnertime and patio-time considering *un*considered roads as curiosity leads us. It's like a "growth spurt" as we stand on six decades of living, knowing we are now positioned to think in new ways, dream new dreams, explore new terrain.

At this moment, I have just hung up the phone after speaking to a woman asking questions about the status of my Addison's disease as she considered our application for nursing-home coverage. When Bob first mentioned such a possibility a few weeks ago, I was appalled! Although he is diabetic and I have Addison's disease—realities that are constant companions—we are in vigorous good health. I couldn't imagine why we should talk to anybody about sending me off to a nursing home. I may be sixty, but in 1991, my heart doctor predicted I'd live to be 109! A nursing home is absurd for us personally, isn't it?

My alarms quieted with the salesman's first words: "It is our goal that you never go to a nursing home. If there are problems in the future, home-care will assist. If either of you do require skilled care, you both would go to the facility of your choice."

My parents did that a generation ago: Mother for seven years, Daddy for two more. With financial help from my brother Joe, they had their own room, their own furniture, their own privacy. I have friends in lovely facilities here where we know we could find happiness if it comes to that. We *want* to stay in this house, in this bed, with these glorious yards until we die. If that is not possible, we can make other choices without causing strain on our children.

We have told our kids, "We did not bring you into the world to let you grow into fulfilling lives to have those lives burdened with your parents' aging!" This policy insures our personal freedom of choice, our independence from the children we love, their independence to continue their own life journeys!

You are forty; I am sixty—but I doubt you would be more stunned than I was when Bob first presented the nursing-home idea to me. But the more we carefully plan for the last third of life, the more this seems to make sense. So we have budgeted it in for monthly payments, praying we never use a dime of the money!

One of our friends is twenty-nine, married, with two children. After a motorcycle accident, he now has to have constant nursing-home care. The horrendous decisions his wife has had to make to create a life with two small children have made us even more aware of how fragile our autonomous security really is. I mention this only because of the timing of this phone call. It seems morbid, some-how. It shouldn't. Our neighbors say they save those monthly pay-ments and they grow to an amount that would care for them into the next decades. We didn't start such a savings program early enough for us to consider this. So we will do it now. This is not morbidity, this is preparation for the unknown.

Bob and I are spending a lot of time, in our sixth decade, begin-ning to make decisions that will enable us to *do life* in the uniquely fulfilling way we now can choose. We are in a place where we would like to dedicate whatever disposable income we have to buy *expe-riences* rather than material things.

I, as a writer, am never happier than when entangled in para-graphs roaming around in my head for clearer ways of expressing my thoughts. As long as I can sit up, have agile fingers and good eyesight, I will want to do that. On the other hand, Bob will soon release his life from the constant daily pressures of administrating his own plumbing, heating, and air-conditioning company. He will sell it this decade. He will not be doing his life-love anymore. So he is planning new things he wants to do with his time, which might include learning to fish, a health-club membership, more time with his beloved electric trains, and, of course, more time on all the me-chanics of our ponds, pools, streams, fountains in our yards, *and* a yen for travel. That time is not yet, but we are carefully considering the new, changing opportunities of *doing life* in our sixties.

And about the seventies, let me tell you: We have friends sev-enty-two and seventy-seven respectively, who have enrolled in more Elderhostel trips than I knew existed. This wonderful travel-study program offers people fifty-five or older a choice of more than two thousand academic institutions in forty-nine countries that offer short-term courses in everything from Advanced Steam Combustion (I made that up for Bob!), Japanese Authors (I made that up for me!), and "The Romance of Archeology," which our friends enjoyed!

I just asked Bob if he would want to do that when we are seventy-two and seventy-five. "We could spend a semester at Oxford!" I enthused. He clapped his hands, exaggerating his delight in going to this prestigious literary institution, which would probably bore him silly. When I explained that if he didn't want to go to Oxford, we could go to the University of Paris, where he could study Advanced Steam Combustion, he shook his head and went to check on the motors in our pools. I don't know if we will do that, but as you consider Columns 70, 80, and 90, you might want to know this is available!

The sculptor Henry Moore said, "The secret of life is to have a task, something you devote your entire life to, something you bring everything to, every minute of the day for your whole life. And the most important thing . . . it must be something you cannot possibly do!" Don't you think he means something we cannot possibly finish in this life but we want to die *trying*?

You wrote, "Moddy, with every fiber of my being I want to *do life*!" I love the concept! I love you! Let's make a pact that every moment, every day, every year, every decade, we will give our finest, fullest, most vital, vibrant energies to *doing life*! Okay?

—Moddy

Facing Mortality at Forty

ANITA HIGMAN

I started to make a tasteless joke about death.
But unfortunately *it isn't . . . a joke.*
Death tends to defy humor.
I have this feeling Moddy isn't afraid of death. I'm terribly curious how she'll answer *the hardest of all human questions.*

. . . . . .

DEAR, SWEET MODDY,

Well, here it is. The biggest of the big. A subject I have been meaning to talk to you about for some time. It's the topic that flattens every effervescent smile at every perfect dinner party.

Death.

I hate this word above all others. It's like I have to give it more room on the page. It demands it. It challenges every living thing. It doesn't stroll in one day like a suitor in a white suit and say, "May I take your hand in death?"

Never. It lunges in, donning a blood brown cape, clawing and devouring. With no apologies. No whisper of reason. Death is no gentleman. He rapes life away forever.

Yes, I know, I am a melancholic temperament, so I can get

particularly graphic when it comes to this subject. (And see how I use humor to deflect the pain of the topic!)

But I do hate death with a passion. I guess I am in good company, though, because even Jesus hated death. And even Jesus wept over it.

But when death steals, will knowing that fact about Jesus be enough to calm the feverish fears in that last breath?

For instance, as you can guess here, I am forty on fast-forward, which gives me a new perspective on this subject. Death is certainly closer than when I was thirty! Yes, I'd say the key word here is closer. Ten years closer. That is a given.

Well, I'd like to change my earthly game selection. I'll take life for one hundred!

Of course, the grave is not only closer at forty than it was at thirty; it seems easier to find its painful and hideous residue. You begin the process by dealing with the passing away of older relatives and friends. This is not an easy life step.

As you well know, my mom died two years ago. I still miss her very much. I wanted to be happy for her that she had found joy in heaven at last, but I still grieve over death's cruelty. It is hard to include joy in this whole scenario, especially after watching her die a slow, agonizing death.

The fatal hour. Sounds like poetry, but it's like all of life's night terrors wrapped up into one unbelievable event. A once-in-a-lifetime happening that we spend the whole of our waking hours trying to put out of our minds. We (I use the plural because I'm just not that different from most people I know!) try to cram our days full, rush here and there, let music fill the silence, and let entertainment anesthetize. I believe some of society's hustle-bustle mania is to forget what is awaiting. The final summons. Total extinction from this side of eternity. Separation like no other.

And, of course, the separation always seems to come too soon.

Moddy, these first forty years went so fast, it's still hard to believe they are past. I'll never be that young girl growing into womanhood again. I'm not only a woman, I'm a woman in the last half of my life! Where did all those hours go? Did they vanish? No. Maybe they got lost in a life rut somewhere.

I mean, you get up, you raise the blinds, you work, you smile, you eat, you clean up, you raise children, you try to do fun things when you can, you close the blinds, and then you go to bed. You get up, you raise the blinds, you work, you smile, you eat, and on and on it goes, until some *thing* gets you, and it's hard to put a lovely slant on that reality.

And what's even spookier is that no one knows how or when it will happen. Death came for a friend of ours as he was sleeping. That might be the least terrifying way to go if you could choose. You remember my friend's husband died instantly in a car crash. There were probably a few seconds of terror. But you can't choose.

Another friend of ours died of cancer. That was not a good way to go. At all. When you think of the terrible pain and agony of cancer or other diseases, perhaps the deterioration adds even more horror to the actual death.

Yes, I'd rather sit this one out. The problem is, I can't wipe the Reaper off my dance card. No one can. It is indeed the last dance, but I'm sure I'd be eyeing the floor for banana peels!

Old joke. It's not really funny. It is just another example of how people try to sugarcoat their true feelings about death.

One problem is that death is so very final. Our minds are simply not set up to comprehend that kind of ending. We go to the movies and maybe we see a lousy ending we don't like. But after a frown and a chuckle we're out into the matinee sunshine starting over with something new. You see, the ending wasn't really an ending. It was fantasy. But death isn't.

Which brings me, Moddy, to yet another angle on this problem.

The spiritual world is real. Not fantasy. I do believe it. But. I have *not* seen it. Some people say they have, but I have not. It is so hard for me to imagine. My flesh has this desperate need to slip my hand into that other dimension. To take just one glorious peek. The older I get the greater that need has come to be. I think it is because we have heard this tiny, nagging voice that says, "Maybe, just maybe there really isn't any more *stuff* out there. The other dimension is really something we've made up out of desperation. This logically may simply be all there is!" Moddy, do you ever wonder if that's possible?

Don't get me wrong, I do believe in the two choices of eternity. I am a Christian, so I am headed to heaven. But the older I get, the more questions I seem to have. And sometimes the questions come out sounding more like doubts.

I know I'm not alone in my fears of aging and dying. That's why I don't see a lot of people talking positively about their own ending. Always there are tears, fears, and gears grinding frantically backward trying to change that infamous time clock in their favor.

The concept is simple. Everyone wants to live. No one wants to die.

I know there have been times when you were a mere breath away from death. Weren't you afraid? *Really?* I've never asked. *Are* you afraid of death? If you aren't frightened about it, how did you come to feel that way? Do you mind talking about it? I hope not. I'd really like to know what is your philosophy of death.

Moddy, I send love to you from someone wanting to grow old with grace and not fear . . . and right now, the word death sounds more hideous than any word on earth!!

—Your own Anita

With Christ You Are Forever Young

RUTH VAUGHN

"I got a letter from Virginia today," I told my son Billy on the phone. "She mentioned Mo-Mo. Do you remember what you said to me when she died? I won't ever forget it, for when you saw my tears, you responded, 'Oh, don't cry! Didn't you know? She was really as young as me all the time. Her body just wore out. It's okay, Mommy.' "

Billy laughed again at the story he had often heard in our church family.

Mo-Mo told the story often. One afternoon my small son sat with her on her porch and asked, "You're awfully old, aren't you?" to which she had responded, "Well, my body is old, but I am still a child! *As young as you!*"

He had looked at her seriously, looking for the joke. "You aren't as young as me! If you were, you could run and jump and ride horses."

Her faded eyes danced. "I suppose I would look rather foolish trying to run or jump or ride a horse now. But it's only my body that is too old. *I* am young!"

My son's brown eyes studied her face. His eyes knit in thought.

She leaned toward him. "I know, I look gnarled and ancient on the outside, but I don't have a gnarled-up, ancient heart! *This body is a sort of a masquerade costume like you wear on Halloween. Inside the costume, I'm still a child! ME! I am still young! I am!* Only my body is old."

"Why don't you get a new one?" he asked with childlike directness.

She smiled softly. "One of these days I intend to do just that!"

"Will you be glad?"

"Oh yes, I'll be glad." Her eyes sparkled. "Then I'll be in heaven, where I can look as young as I feel now . . . where my body will cooperate with the joyousness of youth. Life here is good. Childhood is good; maturity is good; but in the 'larger life' our bodies will wear as long as our spirits. There, with Christ, *I will be forever young!*"

Across phone wires, Billy and I paused to thank God for Mo-Mo's truth.

· · · · · ·

ANITA, MY LOVE,

Let me tell you why I have never been afraid of death. Two words: my mother.

You've gotten to know a lot about her in these letters. The reason is because she impacted my growing life so forcibly in the last decades of her life, when she walked the path of suffering. My father was still in vigorous health, but he retired from his small parish and moved back to the place of their births, Erath County, Texas. They purchased their first new house! It had the first wall-to-wall carpeting, the first central-heating system they had ever known. My brother Joe supplied the air-conditioning and assisted in the purchase of additional acreage behind the house for a huge garden, which was my father's joy.

Mother told me those were, in many ways, the happiest years of their lives, although her health was so frail that Daddy did all the housekeeping, cooked all the meals, and helped her (with walker or wheelchair) to every church service . . . and to frequent picnics and dinners with family who still lived in that area.

Everything about their lives was *new*, and they rejoiced. Daddy no longer pastored a church, but he "pastored" a rest home nearby with weekly services and daily calls. Mother could not go, but she sent notes, flowers, and jars of jams from Daddy's kitchen to the people in the nursing-home parish. She could no longer play the piano, but she still taught piano lessons to children and adults who wanted to learn . . . *free*, of course. It was a time full of happiness. Mother gloried in every moment.

And then it ended.

Daddy called to tell me she was in the hospital. We drove all night to get to her. Every turn of the tires seemed to echo the cry of my heart: "Don't die, Mother. I'm coming. I'm coming."

She was barely conscious of my presence. I had to think she knew unconsciously, for her hand would still wrap itself tightly about mine in the same old way. When we met with the doctor, he assured us she could never return home. She would require special care. That was the first time we had considered a nursing home.

I looked at my father. Fiercely independent, he had cared for Mother's needs alone. He had helped her bathe, helped her dress, combed her hair. He did not want anyone else to interfere. But in the end, he agreed that she must go. My brother Joe came, and as I have shared, he made it financially possible for them to have their own private room, their own furnishings, their own things.

Mother responded to all of the treatment and soon was "herself" again. My father wanted to take her home. But Mother knew her illness had taken its last tenacious hold. She had fought it valiantly through the years, but it was winning. Although remaining in the nursing home meant leaving a dearly loved familiar world and entering a strange new one, my mother was ready to *do life* right there!

She made friends with all the nurses and loved them like her own children. She made friends with the other people in the place and shared pictures of children and grandchildren. Although in a wheelchair, she attended the singing each Tuesday night in the parlor, the Sunday services held by the Christian Church, and visited her friends. (My father continued his "pastoring" in the nursing facility near their home.)

My mother read books, played records, painted small ceramics, worked on scrapbooks for her grandsons, wrote letters, inspected flowers growing in the window, and loved everyone around her.

Then blindness overtook her. She still tried to write to me at least once a week. She wrote in very large letters, and they ambled up and down the page, often into each other . . . but I could make them out! Soon even this was denied her.

In her world of darkness, she listened to the television, had my father help her memorize Scripture and poetry, and enjoyed spelling games and Bible quizzes with anyone who would play with her. When alone, she told me, she would try spelling words backward and quoting poetry backward—just for fun.

And she smiled. To everyone who entered the room, she gave her brightest smile, her interested questions of their lives (she was a *There you are!* person), and her warmest love and promises of prayers. When asked, "How are you?" she, at first, replied, "I'm better, thank you. How are *you*?" My father, acutely aware of her condition, exclaimed one day, "That is a red-hot lie! You are not better! Why don't you tell the truth?" I'll never forget her rueful smile at my father. "Because no one wants to hear it!" He shrugged. "I don't care. Tell the *truth!*" So, Anita, she changed it to, "I hope I'm better, thank you. How are *you*?"

After the first such conversation, she told my father, "*That* is the truth: I hope I'm better. They just want to hear the word better in some context, then they are free to talk about themselves, which, of course, is their first interest." And, of course, my father and I watched her prove its truth. She was the best listener!

As I write this to you today, I understand why I knew at age five that there are two kinds of people in the world. For, you see, I was a *Here I am!* person, but I had observed my mother's determination to focus on others. With a lifetime of practice, she made it an art. In that nursing home, whoever entered her room was received with her delightful, loving, authentic *There you are!* concern for others, yearning to rejoice or weep as needed.

Her indomitable cheerfulness and optimism kept amazing us all. My brother Elton said one time that if we were to leave Mother in a deserted building in the middle of a desert without food and water, she would spend the rest of her life smiling and rejoicing in our love because she would *know* we did it for her own good. As far as we could tell, she never doubted for a moment that the world was a good place, filled with beauty and joy if she only looked in the right places. And she *looked* . . . as long as she could.

Mother lapsed into a coma, where she remained for thirteen months prior to her death. Many times I raced the three hundred miles to the nursing home, expecting to meet the crisis. But her strong heart kept beating.

Early one Saturday morning the phone rang. This time I knew there was no hope. I was afraid I would not be able to get there in time. Somehow I felt I could not bear not to be there. The feeding tubes had been removed. She was receiving no nourishment to sustain her. Her body was rejecting everything. But her heartbeat was strong.

My brothers came, and with our father, we stood by her for six days. Amazingly, her heart kept beating in spite of the lack of food or water. When it ceased, I was standing alone by her bed. "Mother," my heart pleaded, "can't you say something? Please don't leave without saying *something!*" As she drew her last breath, I took a deep breath and felt a sense of peace. She didn't need to say anything now. She had dialogued with me all of my life. It had all been said. Her legacy was mine. It needed no postscripts.

I ran down the hall to the rooms where my brothers were sleeping. They came immediately. Joe went to Daddy, who lay asleep in his bed alongside Mother's. He awakened to Joe's gentle touch. "What's happened?" he asked quickly.

"Mother went to heaven a few minutes ago," Joe said.

My heart constricted. My father had loved my mother in a rare and awesome way. The last years he had waited on her every need with wholehearted devotion. For the last thirteen months, he had watched over her like a mother hen with one chick. I was so afraid he would go to pieces in this moment. But I was not reckoning with the Gibraltar faith and strength of my father. He didn't say anything for a moment. Then he smiled a wistful smile as the tears welled in his eyes. "She's happy."

"Oh, Daddy, yes, she is," said Joe. "If Jesus told us the truth, she is able to see for the first time in months; she is able to run for the first time in years; she is able to sing with the most joyous abandon."

I stood by my mother's still, lifeless body, and my heart whispered, "Oh, God, thank you that I *know* it is not my mother who has died. It is only her shell. She has a new body now *with you*. And no one could ever enjoy it more!"

Daddy said quietly, "I don't know how her heart kept beating for so long."

"We always knew her heart was the most remarkable thing about her," Joe said, smiling through his tears. "Both physically and spiritually."

Oh yes, I thought, *we shall always remember her as a Great Heart!*

The men came from the funeral home. We remained with the body as they prepared it for transfer. I watched as they lifted the stiff legs, which had so long refused to respond to her commands. I saw the flesh on the bedsores tear as they rolled the body, and I *knew* that, although I loved the body she had occupied, it was not *she*. She had been released.

One of the last letters Mother wrote to me in her large scrawling letters spelled out how she wanted me to feel at the time of her death. Here is the letter:

I have been thinking of how close we have been through the years of your life. You came to me, a gift from the hand of God, and I have rejoiced in that gift ever since. We have experienced joy and sorrow, tragedy and triumph together.

But now as I approach the time of my going home, I want to tell you something that you must remember when you are bidding my body good-bye. My child, do not ever say, "Mother is dead." Just know that I'm away; I've gone on ahead to a better land, and one day you will come and we shall again join hands.

Don't think of my sadness at leaving this world where I have known so much joy. Instead, little girl, think of your mother stepping on a shore and finding it heaven; of her taking hold of a hand and finding it God's hand; of her breathing a new air and finding it celestial air; of her feeling invigorated and finding it immortality; of her stepping from storm and darkness and tempest to an unknown calm. Think of your mother waking up and finding it Home.

When we returned from the nursing home that early Friday morning, I took this letter from my suitcase and read it to my family, and we cried. Tears of rejoicing for her; tears of suffering for us.

My brothers and I planned her funeral service. My cousin made her a beautiful pink dress. We selected a bronze casket with soft pink lining. Pink was her color.

Flowers and friends began arriving. I stood long at her casket.

This poem, written on the day of the funeral, expresses the feelings of this daughter as her mother's body lay in state:

February 22, 1971

My mother's body lies in a pink-lined casket.

Her familiar hands are folded;
    her always-smiling face is serene.
People come and say good-bye as if they believe she is dead.
By their tears of finality, I can see
    they have missed the whole point of death.

My mother was full of
    bright life,
    easy laughter,
    quick forgiveness,
    indomitable bravery,
    quicksilver delight.

And when her body wore out, she went away.

Don't you see?

This is not she.

This was her house in which she lived.
This was her set of tools with which she worked.

I love this frail shell lying in the pink-lined casket,
    because she once used those
    hands,
    eyes,
    mouth,
    feet
    to care for me and give me love.

But this is not she.

She is far away.

But all about us still, savoring the new adventure,
    life eternal.
Laughing, caring, relishing, in a dimension

we cannot conceive.

Weep tears of sorrow for our temporary loss,
but do not weep tears of finality,
for we will see her again.

Weep tears of pain at our separation,
but do not weep tears for my mother.

This is her Coronation Day!

My uncle preached the sermon; my oldest brother read her letter to me about death as we gathered around the casket in the cemetery. Her body was laid to rest in the quiet little village of Morgan Mill. On the stone we had inscribed:

Here lies as much Goodness
As can die.

It was a double headstone, for we four children felt those words true of both parents. When we placed my father's body next to my mother's two years later, we had our best lessons in how to face mortality.

When I called the news to my brother Elton, who was a missionary in the Cape Verde Islands, his first words were, "Oh! What will I do now? Wherever I have been in the world, I've always known one thing: Daddy was praying for me!" We wept.

I sat silently in the funeral-home office in America as brother and sister tried to absorb our loss. Finally, I said, "Well . . . as I understand things . . . we children now have to become the patriarchs of the family . . . giving to our children the gifts our parents gave to us. Hard, it is . . . but is this not God's plan for generation following generation?"

When the opportunity came for the two of us, I stood alone before the double grave, while Bob stood quietly aside. My eyes traced the engraved epitaph tenderly and my heart whispered, "We were the Three Musketeers, we were! Now . . . I'm the Only Musketeer! You know how deeply I love you two . . . how fully I thank you for being my parents . . . and oh! . . . I do promise, with my best efforts, to do my best *to make you proud!*"

Anita, my definition of death, phrased in my sixteen-year-old lexicon is: *Open Door Into the Larger Life.*

I believe it. Nothing to fear. Jesus promised, "I have a place prepared" . . . and I believe His words . . . and I believe my mother's words to me, her youngest child, of what I should expect about death. And when the door opens for me, I know I will wake up and find it *Home.*

Oh, dear Anita, let my mother's letter to me be my own letter to you, calming any dread, any anxiety, any fear of mortality. Study her words, accept them as your own from the loving heart of

—Your Moddy

Desiring to Be a More Beautiful Woman at Forty

ANITA HIGMAN

I stared into the mirror once again.
This time I looked even deeper.
I saw just a glimmer of what I had hoped would come someday.
Past my crow's feet, I see a friend . . . and it's me.

I embrace hope, even though my quest isn't complete. I celebrate the *who* of me, even though I am still growing.

I've reached middle age, but it is a daily choice how I will perceive that fact.

Perhaps it's time for me to look up from the mirror gaze and see the eyes of others. There's a whole world of faces to love . . . people I hadn't even noticed before. They have been there all along . . . *just beyond my own reflection.*

· · · · · ·

MY DEAR MODDY,

I want you to know I've soaked up all your letters like parched roses taking on the morning dew. They have become the pretty stream that sprays its mist boldly so near the unknown chasms of life. I am placing each one of your beautiful epistles in a floral box and labeling it "Moddy's Life Letters." Through your words, I have discovered for the first time in my life, the healing beauty of letter writing. It was an island of lost communication for me that has now become an oasis of encouragement and help.

As I ponder all your writings, especially the letters of this last year, I try to grow and learn. As I open the "Moddy Box," I sit on the floor, reading each one over and over. When I've finished the last one, I lie down, close my eyes, and meditate on God's Word, God's love for me, God's celebrating me, understanding the *why and cherishing the who*. And in those silent holy moments, I pray. Oh, Moddy, I know I must face certain life facts and finally try to grow up.

And . . . today, there's this thought I want to share with you.

I know I simply can't keep up. I would like to be beautiful in body, but I see it is indeed a futile cause. Things are beginning to go wrong faster than I can fix them. So I am left with an aging body that I can't totally change. There is no formula to make it perfect again.

Where does that leave me? I guess the truth here is, "I don't want to waste my time trying frantically to preserve what is perishing when I can invest in what will last an eternity!" I want to work on beauty that comes from a smile more than from the perfect shade of lipstick. I want to stop staring at my blue-veined hands and start using them to serve.

The other day I rested on a park bench on a peach-perfect day, thinking of you. I witnessed a scene I must share with you. A grandfather was playing with his granddaughter at the park. He seemed to be in some arthritic pain sitting cross-legged there in the sandbox, but he was more enthralled with the bubbly giggles of his dear one than to worry about his aches. She was coming up with some pretty inventive and wacky stories to go along with her sand animals, and it made her grandfather reel with delight and laughter. His weathered but gentle face was smeared with dirt, and his once neat clothes were wrinkled and sandy. But it didn't seem to matter a bit to him. I saw in his face love and tenderness, and a true giving of himself. The little girl looked into his eyes with such adoration. I watched the scene until my eyes got all misty. It was a moment in time I will never forget, because I believe it is the true essence of your words to me.

My soul longs to have a face that can be looked upon with eagerness, not because of what cosmetics can do, but because the person gazing sees the love of God written all over it. You have made me long for that, because I've seen it in your eyes, and I can read it in your words. And I will never be the same again. Your spirit is mature and lovely and it brings joy to so many people, including me!

There is so much more to do in this life than to focus on myself. I want to be like you and your mother. Not a "Here I am!" kind of person, but a "There you are!" witness to the world.

I can now feel the beginnings of a kind of joy welling up inside of me because I have this longing, and because I do have the assurance it is possible to grow in grace through the years and not simply grow old. Along with the joy, I know there may come pain, but also I can sense a peace in this pilgrimage toward the maturity of my soul. If only I will calm myself and listen to Him who loves me even in my growing up at forty.

I feel a new attitude emerging. And what I mean is, "I want to be more concerned about reflecting Jesus than looking at my reflection."

I ask you this important question, dear Moddy: "How can I grow into the Most Beautiful Woman it is possible for me to be as age advances?"

I want you to know that right now I am weeping with joy at these words. For you have become so precious to me. Thank you for everything. For your twenty years of praying for me, your mentoring me in college as my professor, these glorious letters, the unconditional love as my Moddy dear, and for sharing this wonderful journey called life with me.

Love forever and always, from a woman who wants so much to *make you proud!*

—Your Anita

Let the Beauty of Jesus Be Seen in You

RUTH VAUGHN

I loved my aunt Molly.

But she had face cancer in an era when the malignancy could only be cut away. No reconstructive surgery was possible. The ravages of the surgeon's knife were clear, even leaving an open hole where a tilted nose had been.

But Aunt Molly loved me. She hugged me often, caressing my hair. She laughed at my jokes. She praised my small achievements. She made fluffy biscuits, banana nut bread, and the flakiest cherry pies. I adored Aunt Molly. I wanted to be with her, closely with her, whenever it was possible.

Once at a family gathering, a game was presented where unexpected questions were asked. Each person had to respond instantly. The top-of-the-head answers almost always brought laughter. One time when it was my turn, I was asked, "Name one of the five most beautiful women in the world!"

Without time to think, I answered quickly: *Aunt Molly!*

There was a surprised murmur in the group with much head nodding. Aunt Molly put her face in her hands. I ran to her, afraid I had been wrong. But the tears streaming down her cheeks glowed in the radiance of her face. She held me to her and only whispered two words: "Thank you."

Oh yes, to me, face cancer scars were invisible because Aunt Molly loved me, laughed with me, gave to me. Oh yes, I told the truth that long-ago day: *To me, my aunt Molly definitely was one of the five most beautiful women in the world!*

· · · · · ·

ANITA, MY LOVE,

I slurped every syllable of your letter, pondering how you can grow from age forty into the most beautiful woman possible! We've written many letters in regard to this aging problem we both face. I'm glad it seems we finally agree. Neither of us finds that the best stewardship of our time, energies, and money is to be able to physically age like Lana Turner, Jane Fonda, or Cher! I watched a face-lift surgery and recovery time only last night on television. I decided I didn't want to do that, even if Bob were a millionaire! I'll *do life* with my major time-energy focus on the internal Ruth . . . although I am acutely aware the exterior Ruth has *changed*!

And it hurts, Anita. A few months ago, I was standing in the sun chatting with my son Ron. We were by his car, and in the side mirror I could starkly see *all* the wrinkles, the sagging neck, and I was horrified! Yes, I was. We laughed together while inside my heart screamed, *Oh, Ronnie, can you really look at me now in stark sunlight and still love me with the enthusiasm you did when I was a sleek, beautiful thirty?* Note, it was an interior question. Had I phrased it out loud, I knew what his laughing, teasing response would be. I didn't want to hear it because I knew he loved me *wrinkles and all* . . . so I didn't say anything to him, but my heart resisted my son's *having* to love me *anyway*!!

So, Anita, what do we do?

I have the best answer possible. Honestly, I do.

When I was a child, my mother taught me a small chorus that I sang lustily all my growing years to maturity. Then I forgot it.

In 1986, I remembered it when I was invited to speak for a statewide women's retreat, held near Kansas City, Missouri. The topic they had chosen for my sharing was "Reflections of His Image."

When they sent me a copy of the printed program for those three days, I admired the cover of it. It featured a fancy hand mirror frame with a *real* oval mirror glued in its center! I still consider it perhaps *the* most original program layout for any of my speaking engagements.

Its back cover carried the words I had known a lifetime and forgotten:

Let the beauty of Jesus be seen in me,
All His wonderful passion and purity;
O thou Spirit divine, all my nature refine,
Till the beauty of Jesus be seen in me.

Underneath these lyrics were these, based on 2 Corinthians 3:18:

From glory to glory He's changing me,
Changing me, changing me;
His likeness and image to perfect in me—
The love of God shown to the world.
For He's changing, changing me
From earthly things into heavenly;
His likeness and image to perfect in me—
The love of God shown to the world.

Then followed the chorus:

Turn your eyes upon Jesus;
Look full in His wonderful face,
And the things of earth will grow strangely dim
In the light of His glory and grace.

And then a beautiful butterfly with these words:

Happiness is like a butterfly—

If you chase it,
It eludes you.
If you wait patiently,
It will light on your shoulder.

And the prayer:

"Lord, may your glory be reflected in the happiness of my life!"

Anita, I think this is the answer I would like to give to your letter.

The three days of that seminar were busy. I shared behind the lectern and then in question/answer sessions. The concluding evening service was my performance of an original one-woman play. I remember it well. I pray hundreds of women also treasure the memory of that weekend, but I assure you that the speaker has never been and shall never be the same.

I sang the first chorus unthinkingly, as a child. In 1986 I began to sing it as my heart's deepest prayer. And so it continues today.

In your inimitably passionate way, you ask a vital question for all of us: "How can I grow into the most beautiful woman it is possible for me to be as age advances?" My challenge is that we both agree that in mirror times and in other reflective times, we sing in our hearts or whisper in our house these words:

Let the beauty of Jesus be seen in me,
All His wonderful passion and purity;
O thou Spirit divine, all my nature refine,
Till the beauty of Jesus be seen in me!

Anita, this is our best formula to become the most beautiful women in the world we can be . . . at age forty . . . at age sixty . . . and until we change worlds for a new body and hear Jesus' words: "Well done, thou good and faithful servant!"

From one beautiful woman to another, I send love this day.

—Moddy